Shutters West

A. C. Hull at sixty

Shutters
West

by Nina Hull Miller

Sage Books, *Denver*

© 1962 by Nina Hull Miller

Library of Congress Catalog
Card Number: 62-12404

Sage Books are published by
Alan Swallow, 2679 South York,
Denver 10, Colorado

Dedicated

to my husband

GLENN E. MILLER

for his confidence in me.

Table of Contents

Table of Illustrations

The Photographer

The life of my father, Arundel C. Hull, was not a long one as life spans average today, since he was only sixty-six when he died; but he lived through the stirring years of the Civil War, the building of the Union Pacific Railroad, and the eventful period of great westward emigration. In his boyhood the wars deprived him of his father and two older brothers, but his youth was coincident with the most adventure-filled and excitement-packed period in the history of our country.

Arundel C. Hull was a pioneer photographer. Because of a combination of circumstances, he has not been widely recognized among the early photographers of the West. He made hundreds of pictures through Nebraska, Colorado, Wyoming, and Utah, when they all were territories, beginning in the summer of 1866, when he came west at the age of twenty, until he established a permanent studio at Fremont, Nebraska in January, 1870.

Unfortunately, Hull's name did not appear on the views and portraits he sold in the West prior to the time he began using printed mounting cards with his Fremont gallery address. He died in 1908, before there was a general interest in things relative to the western frontier, and the inadvertent destruction of his large collection of negatives left little trace of his work for archivists to encounter.

Some of Hull's photographic prints have been accredited to his contemporaries whose work was very similar, simply because there was no proof to the contrary. A number of historically interesting pictures will be identified as his among the original prints in this publication which were preserved in an album in his home.

The photographs reproduced here were made by Arundel C. Hull in 1867 and 1868 and antedate any western photographs made by William H. Jackson, dean of early-west photographers, whose hundreds of pictures and paintings made such a graphic contribution to our knowledge of western development.

11

Hull was with Jackson on Jackson's first photograph-making trip west in the summer of 1869, and it is not unreasonable to assume that Hull's two years of previous experience, making pictures over much the same territory, was of considerable value to Jackson.

Arundel C. Hull was born at Fort Wayne, Indiana, on April 14th, 1846, the son of Jacob and Clarissa Arundel Hull. Both of his parents were descended from colonial families of English origin. Jacob's colonial ancestor was George Hull, who came to Massachusetts as a surveyor with the Ludlow Company. Clarissa Arundel was descended from Ezra, a younger son of the Earl of Arundel, who had been kidnapped and impressed on a ship in his youth, and from which he escaped when it reached America.

Both Jacob and Clarissa Hull were born in New York state. Jacob was a silversmith. For a time after their marriage they lived in Pennsylvania. With the surge of emigration toward the Mississippi valley, they moved to Indiana, and then, when Arundel was only a few months old, Jacob went to the Mexican War in a captain's uniform.

According to a carefully preserved letter from her

minister, Clarissa Hull was a woman of unusual character and fortitude, the ideal type of pioneer woman who left family and familiar scenes to go west with her husband and small children, then carried on while her husband went off to war. Jacob Hull was not killed in the Mexican war but died soon after as a result of his service. All too soon Arundel Hull's two older brothers, William Henry Harrison Hull and George Washington Hull, went off to fight in the Civil War. Arundel tried to enlist, too, but was turned away because he was obviously too young and too tall and thin.

One of Arundel's earliest memories was of his father coming home from the Mexican war and bringing him, in his pocket, a baby black squirrel. Clarissa Hull lost her husband and two sons to the wars and still carried on while she lost three more children one by one from the diseases that took large numbers from the early settlements, and she was left with only the youngest, Arundel.

At the age of fifteen Arundel became interested in the relatively new and complicated art of photography. There was a pronounced artistic strain in his ancestry which he inherited and photography offered an outlet for his talent which was practical enough for making a living. When he was sixteen he went to Saint Paul, Minnesota, where he worked in a gallery for a year learning portrait photography. It promised to be an absorbing and challenging profession, for in the 1860's a photographer had to be something of a chemist as well as an artist and mechanic.

Saint Paul was a fascinating place for a young man in 1862. Hull was often at the docks, watching the river-front activity; and a natural outcome was a yearning to make a picture-taking trip south by river steamer. It was at the docks that he became friends with James J. Hill, several years his senior, who was a shipping clerk and who later became the great railroad magnate. Hill had returned from the east coast where he had worked for a time trying to get enough money together for passage to Europe. When he finally had to give up, he returned to Saint Paul. J. J. Hill was so sincerely excited over developments in the West and the opportunities he was sure could be found there, it is quite probable that his enthusiasm had something to do with his young friend Hull's losing interest in a river trip.

Working under the photographer in Saint Paul, Hull became an expert portrait photographer. An opportunity came to open a gallery of his own at St. Cloud, Minnesota, and since by then his mother was the only member of his family living, she accompanied him there. The responsibility of a new business was a diversion from the go-west fever that was becoming more and more impelling.

Although Hull was only seventeen when he established this first studio in 1863, he had somehow obtained by then more education than was common at the time, for in later years his children found him to be familiar with the classics and great operas and well grounded in Latin, history, and mathematics.

Before the first year had passed in St. Cloud, Clarissa Hull died of the disease so common then, conjestion of the lungs, which is now known as tuberculosis. It was in the dead of winter and the snow was too deep for horses to travel. There was no railroad nearer than Saint Paul. In order to get his mother's body back to Fort Wayne for burial in the family plot, this eighteen-year-old boy did the only possible thing—placed it on a hand sled and pulled

A. C. Hull at 17 when he
established his first photo gallery

A. C. Hull, 1867-8, age 21

14

the sled seventy-five miles to the railroad.

Hull remained in business in St. Cloud for about three years. A. C. Hull, Photographer, was still listed in the Minnesota Business Directory in 1865. Of his years there the memory of the Red River Carts stayed with him most clearly all his life. Like the river steamboats, they spelled adventure and the weird sound they made could not be forgotten, much less duplicated anywhere. He described to his children the unearthly shrieking of the ungreased wooden wheels of a hundred and fifty two-wheeled carts, ringing for miles through the crisp cold air. Each pulled by a single ox or Indian pony, the long procession of Red River Carts came down from hundreds of miles north in what is now Canada, at the end of the hunting season. Each was piled high with several hundred pounds of furs and pemmican. No grease could be used to deaden the creaking wail that ran the whole range of sound, because it would collect so much dust the wheels could not turn.

The year was 1866, and, after the close of the Civil War, the attention of the people and the government had again turned toward the development of the West. It seemed to a young Hoosier lad that every young fellow he talked to was ambitious to seek out a location in the vast territory opened up by the Louisiana Purchase, or to stake out a mining claim in the mountains. There was also the exciting fact that a railroad was actually being built westward from Omaha.

His desire to see the West could no longer be held down. Hull sold his gallery, home, and all his possessions except the oil portraits of his mother and father and a few family papers and photographs. These with a few keepsakes he left with a cousin for safekeeping. Then he prepared a box covered with black cloth in which he fitted his photographic equipment so that he could develop and print pictures anywhere. With his personal effects packed in a portmanteau that had a lithograph of a New England scene in the lid (it remained in the attic of his home until he died), he was ready to see the country he and J. J. Hill had spent so many hours speculating about.

Hull was twenty years old, six feet tall with black hair and very blue eyes and the slender build he retained throughout his life. He was free to go anywhere and make expenses as he went. But the family

15

doctor made a dire prediction that, since he had cared for his mother during her illness, he would not live until his twenty-first birthday. There was a possibility that the newfangled notion of living outdoors might prevent an early demise, and the climate of Colorado was said to be good for "lungers," but the doctor did not offer much encouragement. Hull went ahead with his plans and he was never sick in bed a day in his life until about a year before he died of a heart attack.

Arundel Hull reached Omaha in the summer of 1866 and set about making pictures of street scenes and buildings, finding he could easily sell all the prints he made. Time was of no importance, a winter in Omaha would be sure to bring interesting experiences; so he found a job as a portrait photographer. It was in the gallery of E. L. Eaton, who had established the first studio in Omaha, had then gone off to the Civil War, and had just returned to resume his business.

The winter passed swiftly and in the spring Hull left Omaha for the mountains. The remainder of 1867 and nearly all of 1868 he spent in Colorado, Wyoming, and Utah Territories, during which time he made the

photographs in the collection reproduced in this volume. Late in the fall of 1868 he returned to Omaha, where he found a new gallery in operation—Jackson Brothers. Hull went to work for them as portrait photographer.

In the spring Jackson Brothers secured a contract from the Union Pacific Railroad Company for a thousand stereotype photographs of scenes along the new railroad. William H. Jackson and Arundel C. Hull left Omaha on May 22, 1869, to spend the summer fulfilling this contract. Jackson worked until September, then returned to Omaha. Hull remained until December to fininsh up the work, then resumed the portrait work in the Omaha gallery for the remainder of the year.

Hull's part in the making of the now famous Union Pacific pictures was never acknowledged except for a brief mention in Jackson's books, *The Pioneer Photographer* and *Time Exposure,* since Jackson had the contract and the two lost contact with each other soon after. In a letter to the writer several years before his death, William H. Jackson wrote, "Along the Union Pacific that summer, your father assisted me in all my photographic work, sometimes doing it alone."

FR

on

ets.

also

as

A. C. & HULL,

Photographer

FREMONT, NEB.

INDIAN, PICTURES.

Views of the Union Pacific Railroad.

Views of Residences and Business Houses taken to order.

Old Pictures Copied and Enlarged, and colored in Oil India Ink, or Water colors

ts.

and
im

The

Fremont Weekly Herald
Feb. 9, 1876

Fremont, Nebraska, 331 Main Street

17

Hull established his second studio at Fremont, Nebraska. He built a building at 331 Main Street and opened for business on January 1, 1870. It was probably the first permanent photograph gallery in Nebraska outside Omaha. He became well known for the quality of his work and many of his portraits are to be found in family collections throughout eastern Nebraska. They are artistic even by modern standards and show technical skill that must have been hard to achieve at the time.

About 1895 Hull sold his business to Fritz and Good. Later W. P. Fritz operated it alone until about 1910, but the building remained the property of the Hull family. The business changed hands two or three times before the building was torn down in 1928, but it still was called by many people the Old Hull Gallery.

Hull prized his old negatives and felt that pictures of pioneer days would sometime be of special interest. In the back room of his studio he stored hundreds of boxed and labeled glass plate negatives. Many were priceless, as for instance the negative of the first photograph Sitting Bull ever allowed anyone to take

of him. The negatives of the scenes Hull had taken in the mountains in 1867 and 1868 were there, many portraits of early settlers of prominence, Indian chiefs, views of Indian villages, frontier events and celebrations, buildings, homes, and institutions.

One of the later owners of the business was either ignorant of the value of Hull's collection of negatives or was indifferent. Unknown to the family and other persons who would have been concerned, he had the whole lot hauled to the dump. By the time the distressing fact was known it was too late to do anything about it.

After Arundel C. Hull had sold his photograph business because he felt the darkroom work was becoming too confining, he served for a number of years as Fremont's first water and light commissioner. For the last eight years of his life he was Midwest sales manager of the fire apparatus department of the Manhattan Rubber Company. He was in Chicago to confer with the general manager about a promotion when he died of a heart attack in his sleep, on December 30, 1908. The day before, he had taken a trip to Fort Wayne, Indiana, to see if the family plot in the cemetery there was being properly cared for.

19

Hull's life was typical of the early day business men who helped the progress of their towns in any way they could. A file of the Fremont *Herald* for the 1870's and 1880's contains many items about A. C. Hull, his activities and his family, and honored him as a public-spirited citizen. In 1880, when his gallery was ten years old, he had the building moved back on the lot and a new section built on the front of it. The *Herald* said:

> July 15, 1880—A. C. Hull will open his new photograph gallery on Thursday. It is one of the most convenient in the West and is furnished in splendid style. It is a credit to our city.

> July 29, 1880—A. C. Hull has just completed a telephone line running from his residence to his gallery. We don't propose to let him take our picture on any such scheme as that.

Hull's photographs consistently took first premiums at the county fair where all artistic displays were housed in Floral Hall. The *Herald* editor was generous in his praise:

> Oct. 10, 1877—One of the most attractive

features of Floral Hall is the large display of handsome pictures from A. C. Hull's gallery and if he does not carry away an armful of premiums it will not be bacause he does not deserve them.

The famous painter Thomas Moran, whose early oil paintings have always been most highly valued, and for whom Mount Moran was named, was a guest at the Hull home while he spent several days looking through Hull's mountain scenes and selecting those that would be of help to him in his work.

Hull was an ardent and staunch Republican and one of his favorite pastimes was discussing politics across the alley fence with Doctor Abbott, father of writer Keene Abbott and the artist Osie Abbott. Dr. Abbott was a Democrat. As their arguments grew hotter, the voices of the two men grew louder and louder until someone in the neighborhood managed a timely interruption. The Abbott family lived in a big sprawling house that had earlier been occupied by the Dr. Borglum family whose sons Gutson and Solon became two of the world's greatest sculptors.

Although from his youth Hull was extremely interested in territorial, state, and national politics, he would never consent to run for office himself; but he enjoyed making frequent campaign speeches for others in the towns around Fremont. He was on the debating team of the Prairie View Literary Society which carried on a series of lively debates on timely subjects with literary groups of other towns. He and his family were members of St. James Episcopal Church, founded by the Reverend Orsamus C. Dake, one of the West's earliest poets.

One of the charter members of Signet Chapter No. 8 Royal Arch Masons and of Fremont Lodge No. 859 Knights of Honor, Hull consistently held office in these and the Knights Templar. He was one of the Fremont Social Club, with membership limited to thirty-five men.

Of a number of subscription lists in which Hull's name appeared were those to start a creamery and to build a bridge over the Platte River. In 1861 he was one of a group of men who subscribed to a fund to establish Fremont Normal School, which is now Midland College. The Fremont *Herald* said that the prospects for a school looked favorable since a number of business men had interested themselves in raising the sum required. Hull held office in the Fremont Board of Trade and Commercial Club, the forerunners of the modern Chamber of Commerce. He was an advocate of good roads and was consistently on the Good Roads Committee.

At a celebration in 1883 Hull was honored as one of the originators of the Fremont Volunteer Fire Department and of the Frontier Hook and Ladder Company. Membership in one of the early day firefighting companies depended to a degree on social standing. There was great rivalry between the teams as to the excellence of their performance and contests were held at the annual state meetings. Hull seems usually to have had some official capacity at the annual Firemen's Ball, one of the most important social functions of the year and an elaborate costume affair when the committees were decked out in wide satin badges topped with large velvet rosettes to indicate their official status.

Hull was one of the organizers of the Nebraska State Firemen's Association and was president of the organization in 1901. In 1904 he was elected vice-president of the National Volunteer Firemen's Association at the annual meeting in St. Louis.

Omaha—1866-1868

Arriving in Omaha in the summer of 1866, everything he encountered was new to a young Hoosier photographer, and Arundel Hull was amazed and fascinated by the enormous activity in the "Gateway to the West." The air fairly smelled of adventure. Miners and speculators were gathering their supplies and outfits, tense with excitement over every word of new strikes in the mountains, eager to be off to Utah or the Clear Greek gold mines of Colorado. Emigrants were outfitting themselves and their prairie schooners, then assembling on the mosquito-ridden miry flat at the foot of California Street until groups of a hundred or so wagons were ready to start west together.

Soldiers and freight trains of military supplies were being dispatched to the forts established by the government throughout the territories for protection from the Indians. On the outskirts of town were the freighter camps where ox and mule teams were corralled and where the bull-whackers and mule-skinners made camp while the wagons of the great freight trains were being loaded.

There was much to see at the Missouri River wharf where the light-draft, stern-wheeler craft from the south unloaded all sorts of cargo, including rails for the new railroad. The daily steamboat from St. Louis brought more westbound travelers to add to the constant stream of people coming and going through Omaha, the stepping-off place for the western trails.

Omaha had been seeing this activity for ten years, and yet it was just a beginning, for the town lay directly in the path of westward travel, an advantage recognized by the small group of men who had purchased the site from the Omaha Indians. For ten dollars they had acquired a thousand and fifty-five acres of the Indian's hunting ground, had founded a town, and had given it the Indian name.

In all the hustling activity of the fall of 1866 there was a great deal to attract a young man with a camera, and although Hull still felt the magnetic pull of the mountains, he decided to stay in Omaha until spring, when more miles of railroad would have shortened the great stretch of stagecoach travel necessary to reach the Rockies. The Union Pacific was actually under construction west of Omaha.

It was an eventful winter. In January the Northwestern Railroad from Chicago was completed to the eastern side of the Missouri River opposite Omaha and the first train from the east was welcomed with an appropriate celebration. On March first, following months of speculation and political pulling and hauling, Nebraska Territory was admitted to the Union as a state. The state capitol was designated as Lincoln, although there had been several unsuccessful attempts to move the Territorial capitol from Omaha to other locations, and Omaha had tried in vain to keep it. Lincoln then became, in the words of one cynical historian, the "seat of Legislative wisdom and Legislative folly."

Hull's photography kept him busy and was profitable, and it is a pity more of his pictures of this period in Omaha cannot be identified. But his stay in Omaha was valuabe to him in other ways. The experience of being where the political aspects of the building of the Union Pacific and the admission of the Territory of Nebraska as a state were discussed on every side, stimulated his life-long interest in politics.

Before long Hull was offered a job in the photograph gallery of E. L. Eaton, doing the portrait work for which he was trained. In spare time he continued his street scene photography and made the pictures shown here.

The business boom that was underway in Omaha in 1866 was later refered to as Omaha's epoc of extreme prosperity. A number of brick buildings were under construction. All of them were not completed that year, but they were giving the town an air and were described at the time as "the superior class of elegant brick buildings." Hull photographed the Ware Block, watched the Central Block go up, and photographed it completed on his return from the mountains in 1868.

The Central Block was a full block long and three stories high, on Farnam Street between Thirteenth and Fourteenth. It was built by Milton Rogers, whose Stove Store occupied the corner. The other stores in the building were mostly wholesale businesses and

Ware Block, Omaha, showing signs: J. C. Mackey & Co.
    Tootle and Co., Dry Goods   J. A. Ware and Co., Bankers
    John McCormick and Co.   E. L. Emry Real Estate

Central Block, Omaha, showing following signs:

M. Hellman and Co.

Kurtz, Mohr and Davis

Barney Bros.

Wolcott and Co.

Central Nat'l Bank

Ketcham and Burns

Stephens and Wilcox

Excelsior Stoves

some of those whose signs are visible in Hull's photograph continued in operation for many years.

The Ware Block at the corner of Thirteenth, on the north side of Farnam, had been built by the Ware Company Bank the year before Hull made his photograph. The Ware Bank occupied the corner section of the two-story building for four or five years. Other banks occupied it in turn over a long period.

Next to the bank was the wholesale liquor store of J. C. Mackoy and Company. Third was John McCormick and Company, wholesale grocers. Last, in the opposite corner from the Ware bank, was M. Tootle and Company, wholesale drygoods, boots and shoes. A great deal of activity centered around the Ware Block because these wholesale establishments did a huge business with freight trains out of Omaha.

Behind the Ware building, on Thirteenth Street between Farnam and Douglas, stood the first Methodist Church to be built in Omaha. There was a vacant lot next to it, to the rear of the Mackoy and McCormick stores. This lot and the alley were jammed with freight wagons on Sunday mornings while Mackoy and McCormick loaded their customers' purchases.

Sunday was the day all freighters except the Mormons loaded up for an early start on Monday.

The freighters, ranchmen, and traders who periodically came to town with their pouches of gold dust and nuggets, furs and soldier's checks, would be weary of the city by Sunday and ready to load up. The resulting hullabaloo behind the little church was a most inharmonious combination of cracking whips, creaking wagons, banging, scraping, and rattling, peppered with the bellowing oaths of the bullwhackers and mule-skinners.

All this went on almost under the windows of the little church and often it was doubtful if Elder Smith could shout loud enough to be heard over the din outside. His loyal congregation claimed he usually accomplished it, but at least once he was exasperated beyond control, stopped in the middle of his sermon, and went out to protest. Shouting at the loudest shouters in what he termed a pleasant way, he had satisfactory and more or less lasting results.

The International Hotel, where Hull first stayed when he arrived in Omaha, was an imposing four-story brick hostelry with a hundred sleeping rooms. It was built for $70,000 in 1858 at the northeast cor-

International Hotel, Omaha, 1867

ner of Ninth and Farnam. Originally The Herndon House, it was so named in honor of a heroic young Navy officer whose exploration of the upper Amazon brought him fame before he lost his life on a storm-wrecked ship off the coast of Panama. It was built as a boom hotel and during its early years many interesting happenings took place there and it was the scene of many of Omaha's most gala social affairs. Balls were held there with all pomp and dignity, the guests bidden by engraved invitations. But since the hotel had no regular chef in the kitchen, the ladies in their elaborate, bustled gowns furnished and served the repast.

In 1867 part of the lower floor of the International House was occupied by the Union Pacific ticket office and general freight office, and the ticket offices of the Western Stage Line and the General Stage Line. These were at the end or Ninth Street front, where, in the days of The Herndon House there was a door designated by a sign as the Ladies Entrance. The stanch old building was not demolished until 1922.

The diningroom of the International was still being used for balls when Hull arrived in Omaha. Dramatic

performances and local theatricals had been held there and more recently in the Court Room on the second floor of the Court House. But that winter of 1866-1867 Hull saw stock company plays in Omaha's first real theater. One of the stock companies must have failed to give passes to the editor of *The Weekly Herald,* for he said in his paper:

> Don't throw away your money by attending such a farcical humbug.

Hull's general view of Omaha, taken from an upper window of Senator Millard's house at Seventeenth and Farnam, shows the front of the Court House, an attractive, two-story red brick colonial style building that was erected in 1857. It stood at Sixteenth Farnam on the northeast corner of the block known as Washington Square until it was cut up into lots and sold.

Facing the Court House, on the other side of Sixteenth Street, was a little brick church with a beautiful white spire, the first protestant church to be erected in Omaha. Another of the early hotels can be seen in Hull's picture, to the left of the church spire. The Hamilton House was on Douglas Street between

Omaha, Nebraska, in 1868

Sixteenth and Fifteenth Streets, ten years old when Hull made the photograph. West of the Court House the higher part of the townsite was beginning to develop into a select residential section with a few fine homes on the terraced hillsides.

Not all of Omaha's first buildings were of such lasting credit as those Hull photographed. One brick building at 1008 Farnam maintained its equilibrium with dignity for several years then suddenly fell down of its own weight, burying an actress from the town's first theater. She was rescued with much solicitude without having suffered any serious injury. The publicity may have been worth the experience.

Westward

In the early spring of 1867 Hull repacked his black box of photographic equipment and again headed west, enjoying the luxury of train travel as far as the railroad was finished. It was not all new country to him, however. During the winter he had made several short trips to Nebraska towns. Some of these were tours or excursions promoted by the railroad company for publicity.

Typical of the stations established by the railroad every twelve miles along the right of way was Elkhorn Station, twenty-eight miles from Omaha. The area around it was already recognized for its fertile soil as well as for the quantities of wild game in the Elkhorn valley and fish in the river. The natural resources of this river were augmented in the early 70's when a carload of fish, intended to stock a California stream, was accidentally dumped into it while the tank was being refilled with river water.

When the picture was taken the first house had yet to be built at Elkhorn Station. There were the necessary section house, freight depot, and water tank with windmill. These, with later a few cabins and a general store, were usually all to be found at the sites designated by the railroad company on their land-grant sections. They continued to be called Stations unless a town grew up and the settlers either changed the name or dropped the Station. Some of them did ultimately become towns or cities, others disappeared entirely, and some have remained very little changed.

In contrast to the towns that sprang up ahead of the railroad construction, and the stations established by the railroad, were Fremont, Columbus, and Grand Island, Nebraska. They were laid out and settled in Nebraska Territory, well in advance of the coming of the Union Pacific, by town companies whose members chose the sites for permanent homes.

Fremont was platted in 1856, and the settlers immediately began to plan for future permanent improvements so that it had been a steadily growing

Elkhorn Station, Nebraska

Fremont, Nebraska, in 1867

town for ten years before the railroad arrived. The financial crash of 1857 had sent some of the town company back east and cramped somewhat the enterprise of those who weathered it through, but the discovery of gold in the Rocky Mountains during Fremont's second year increased emigration through it and gave it a second start. That year an event that showed the determination of the settlers was the founding of St. James Hall, an Episcopal Seminary, by the Reverend Orsamus Charles Dake. Dake was one of the West's earliest poets, whose work includes legends of the Otoe and Omaha Indians.

One of the most important of the Overland Stage Stations in the Platte valley had been for years a point near the junction of the Loup River with the Platte about a day's stagecoach ride from Omaha. The town of Columbus was started near it in 1856 by a group organized in Omaha that had the distinction of having a woman cook. It was a thriving settlement from the first and was incorporated by a special act of the Territorial Legislature in 1865, a year before the railroad came. Photographer Hull was impressed with the future prospects of Columbus, as he had

been with Fremont, and considered them both for permanent location later on.

Around the site of Columbus the agricultural tribe of Pawnee Indians raised corn and pumpkins in the Loup and Platte valleys. They were friendly to the whites, and the railroad company had asked the government to recruit a company of Pawnee Scouts to help protect the surveys being made across the plains. The command of the company was given to Major Frank North and several young subordinate officers of Columbus. North was one of the earliest settlers there. He and his company played an important role in controlling the plains Indians and protecting the railroad line. Hull encountered the Scouts several times going to the mountains and returning, including their camps in his photographs.

The picture of the wagon bridge over the Loup Forks was made on Hull's return trip from the mountains. It was the interesting result of a sort of evolution in stream crossing at this point where it was necessary to cross either the Loup or the Platte to go on west. For the first five years emigrants and freight trains had forded the river, quite deep most of the year. Then an enterprising settler rigged up a ferry,

Bridge over Loup Forks at Columbus, Nebraska

Grand Island, Nebraska, in 1867

using a common rope for motive power. In a few years a cable ferry was put into use. In 1863 the ferry was replaced with a pontoon bridge. When the real bridge of Hull's photograph was built it was considered a wonderful piece of construction.

One of the early buildings of interest shown in Hull's photograph of Grand Island is the O K Store owned by Koenig and Weibe. Built in 1862, it had been moved into town from its original location about a mile south, in 1867, shortly before the picture was taken. During the Sioux and Cheyenne War, while still on the original site, it had been fortified with corner rifle towers and walled with a breastwork of sod as a refuge for the overflow of settlers who could not be accomodated in the stockade in Grand Island.

The Roman Catholic Church, which can also be seen in the photopraph of Grand Island, was built soon after the town was laid out but was blown down in a storm four years after and had to be rebuilt. It was at the corner of Second Street and Walnut. The first settlers of Grand Island were a large group of Germans from Iowa who recognized the advantages of the location in the center of a large area of fertile land. They were prepared to wait for the time when they would have transportation to market for their products, and, like Fremont, Grand Island was a going concern before the railroad reached it.

On across Nebraska

The photograph Hull took of Plum Creek is probably the only one there is of the original town, which later became Lexington. The Plum Creek Pony Express Station was established in 1860 on the south side of the Platte River a few miles from where a stream by that name flows into it. The next year Mr. and Mrs. Daniel Freeman built a store across the road, calling it the Plum Creek Store. In 1863, in anticipation of the coming of the railroad, the Freemans filed on a section of land on the north side of the river and moved their store there, still calling it the Plum Creek Store.

The Plum Creek Store was well known to travelers on the Oregon Trail. Mrs. Freeman, during the busy months, baked a hundred pounds of flour into bread every day and sold it to the emigrants for fifty cents a

loaf. When the Union Pacific came through, a railroad section house was built on the Freeman land by mistake because, in 1866, the government survey had been completed only as far as Kearney. The settlement that grew up around the station was called Plum Creek Station and many times the settlers found refuge from the Indians there. When the survey disclosed the error in location, the railroad company moved the section house to land owned by the Union Pacific one mile to the west. In 1872, about five years after the picture was made, the town followed to the permanent site, which is now Lexington.

Plum Creek seemed serene and safe enough when Hull first saw it in 1867, but the name was reminiscent of the Plum Creek Massacre which occurred a few miles from the station in 1864, when a wagon train of four mule teams had been attacked and all eleven people in the party killed and scalped by Indians. Before Hull's return from the mountains, another incident occured which brought Plum Creek Station into historical prominence. The Indians succeeded in wrecking a train near there on July 7, 1867. A band of Southern Cheyennes, led by Chief Turkey Leg, pried up the rails at a point a few miles west

Plum Creek with soldiers encamped

of the station, piled ties under them, and used some of the telegraph line to tie them fast. A handcar carrying three men struck the obstruction first and was thrown into the ditch. One of the men was killed and another crawled away in the dark. The third was scalped, and his scalp is preserved in the Union Pacific Museum in Omaha.

The engineer of the train that followed the handcar was unable to stop the train and the engine and cars piled up. He and the fireman were burned to death. The conductor escaped in the dark and flagged a second train, returning with it to Plum Creek Station. At daylight, when a trainload of settlers approached the wreck, the Indians had fired the box cars after looting them and were riding around the prairie with long bolts of bright-colored calico tied to their pony's tails, flying like banners in the wind. The engine involved in the memorable train wreck was called the Osceola.

Hull's photograph of Plum Creek Station shows the tents of Major North's Pawnee Scouts, who were detailed to the area to ward off further threats of Indian attacks. The building to the left is the Plum

Creek Store, a two-story building with store and living quarters on the ground floor. Wood-choppers who supplied the railroad with fuel lodged above. Mr. Freeman was a freighter and his wife began running the store alone in 1862, continuing after her husband was drowned in the river. In the photograph the section house is nearest in the foreground.

Willow Island was a telegraph and passenger station and, like Plum Creek Station, was situated where the bluffs across the river made excellent cover for marauding Indians. In addition, a heavy growth of willows on the islands in the Platte protected the savages while they made raids on the stock of the settlers. The first board-and-log houses at Willow Island were walled up with bullet-proof sod, pierced on each side with rifle holes. Hull's picture of the section house and windmill at Willow Island was taken from the top of a box car.

Windmills such as this one are in evidence in several of Hull's photographs. The windmills came with the railroad. At every station, and close to the tracks, stood the squarish wooden tank on a tall structure, surmounted by a circle of fan blades. These mills derived their power from the ever active prairie

Railroad shops at North Platte

winds, to pump water for the locomotives and station houses. They were automatically regulated by a floating globe that shut off the mill when the tank was full. Since all of Hull's photographs were time exposures, all his windmills show the path of the moving fan blades. The mills were visible for miles, marking the line of the railroad at twelve-mile intervals. Curiously, the tanks of water, exposed to the bitter winter weather and winds of the plains, never froze.

At North Platte, Hull found railroad shops and a roundhouse under construction. A startling contrast to the large brick structures were the tepees of a band of Sioux at the edge of town. The Indians let him take photographs and a good many prints were easily sold. The finished railroad shops and roundhouse he photographed the following year, and then he heard how the shops had scarcely been completed when the threat of an Indian attack sent all the settlers skurrying into them for protection. Many times along the railroad the roundhouses proved to be the safest refuge in time of danger.

The North Platte railroad shops were a boon to the settlers in another quite special way. An accomodating engineer rigged up a bathhouse where all the townspeople were free to enjoy hot or cold baths. Probably the settlers who took advantage of the privilege would not have agreed with the historian who said that the railroad shops at North Platte cost $300,000 but were not worth three cents to the railroad company, being merely one of the many requirements of the government which greatly increased the cost of building the road.

The country at the forks of the Platte was even then, in 1867, showing signs of becoming a great cattle-raising area where the rich prairie grasses had made it a favorite hunting ground of the plains Indians. A military post was being constructed there that year. It was at North Platte that Hull first saw *The Frontier Index*, the newspaper popularly called "The Press on Wheels."

A pair of brothers, Fred K. and Leigh R. Freeman, were the editors of a unique, forceful, but short-lived newspaper that moved along ahead of the railroad construction. *The Frontier Index* was begun at Doby Town near Fort Kearney after the close of the Civil War. It was produced on a printing outfit

Union Pacific Station, Willow Island, Nebraska, 1867

Sioux tepees at North Platte

hauled on a wagon from place to place, sometimes staying a year in one spot. It reported with extreme candor every event of interest, and attacked lawlessness, crime, and criminals fearlessly and without restraint. The column of local news items gave a frank picture of life in the new towns, progress of the railroad was reported week by week, and the frequent deaths by violence were given no more attention than any other news item.

When *The Frontier Index* moved from Doby Town, it paused briefly at Plum Creek, North Platte, Julesburg, Fort Sanders, Laramie, Benton, Green River, and Bear River City, as it followed the railroad across the plains. At Bear River City in Utah Territory in November, 1868, a rioting mob burned the jail, and because the *Index* had always been an advocate of law and order, the rioters burned the building in which it was housed also.

Typical of the news items *The Frontier Index* carried was this:

March 24, 1868—The headquarters of the Union Pacific are established at Fort Steele. We have just landed from Cheyenne without a break in our neck and free from bullet holes but there are six youths down there breathless and speechless since Friday last. . . . Two hanged by Vigilantes Friday night; three shot on Sunday evening before nine o'clock and four others reported wounded the same night.—The people of Cheyenne are determined to have law and order or break a hame-string in the attempt.

Until the railroad company built a bridge across the Platte River near North Platte in the fall of 1866, one of the main fords on the overland trails was at this point. Here the river was wide, but shallow, except at certain seasons of the year. But although the depth of the water was not usually formidable, the ever-shifting quicksands of the river bottom made it a treacherous fording.

The railroad bridge was built on wooden piles and in order that it could be used for wagons and stock, the railroad company floored it with planks and rented it to Lincoln County. It was a long bridge, 2600 feet, entirely without protection at the sides, and most horses and mules had to be led across. A bridge-watcher, stationed in a cabin near one end, was required to walk the full length of the bridge

North Platte Bridge

after the passage of every train. Hull's photograph shows that short poles attached along one side of the bridge carried the telegraph wires.

The tracks were laid into Julesburg, Colorado Territory, in June of 1867 and in the night a large portion of North Platte was loaded on flat cars and transported there. In twenty-four hours Julesburg was a town and the new terminus of the railroad. But it was doomed from the start. After less than six months of doubtful glory it was moved bodily to Cheyenne.

Into Wyoming Territory

Hull made his leisurely way from town to town across Nebraska only a few months after it was made a state. To a lad who had grown up in an old settled part of the country, where substantial homes were made of wood, logs, or brick, the makeshift houses on the prairie were curiously uninviting. Across the new state the scarcity of lumber became more and more apparent, but the dobies, soddies, and dugouts developed by the resourcefulness of the settlers were ingeniously suited to their needs. Because of their use the plains country was settled much more quickly than might have been.

With walls laid up of blocks of buffalo sod, or whatever tough grass was native to the spot, and sod roofs over a framework of poles, the soddies defied the bitter winter winds and provided homes that were snug and warm. They were cool in summer, too, and the walls were bulletproof. Usually only one room with a hard-packed earth floor, they took no money outlay except for a door, a chimney pipe, and a window or two. The best type of sod house was like the one Hull photographed at Ogallala, a frame structure walled up with sod on the outside. Naturally the occupants of this one posed in front of it and no doubt a picture was sent "back east" for the home folks to see.

Between the first time Hull saw Ogallala in 1867 and his return from the mountains late in 1868, a history-making development had taken place and it had become a great cattle-shiping point for the vast herds of Texas longhorns driven up from the south. Along with the Chisholm Trail, Ogallala became a setting for cow-country legend and song, both true and fictitious, which accented a particular brief chapter in the history of the West. The great cattle drives were the background for daring and heroic deeds of strong men at their best, as well as for the ruthlessness and violence of men at their worst.

Already a rough railroad terminus, the drive herders added to the turmoil that gave Ogallala the repu-

48

Mud house at Ogalalla, Nebraska

tation of a wild town with restless people. It was indeed the wildest town Hull had yet seen, the construction workers and cowboys involved in many an incident, but it was only an initiation for what he was to see later. At Ogallala Hull was near to the end of his travel by train. He could go on to Sidney and Pine Bluffs and then must take a stagecoach.

By August, Sidney was a sub-division of the new railroad, fifty miles from the line between the new state of Nebraska and Wyoming Territory. Hull must have been uncertain where the line was, for he wrote on the back of his photograph, Sidney, Wyoming Territory. It was a much better built town than the average station or tie camp. The roundhouse here was welcomed by the settlers as a safe place when Indians threatened to attack. Trainloads of rock were quarried from the hillsides at Sidney for ballast for the tracks. Preparation was being made for building army barracks and government storehouses for military supplies. The pile of railroad ties in the background of Hull's photograph was nearly half a mile long.

Sidney retained the characteristics of a railroad

terminus longer than others where the activity ended when the track was finished. Daily stagecoaches ran from Sidney to the gold mines in the Black Hills, adding miners and prospectors to the motley mixture of plains characters. Indians continued to attack as late as April, 1869. Murders and deaths in drunken brawls were so common little attention was given them.

Arundel Hull's photograph of Pine Bluffs, Wyoming Territory, is an interesting study of the types of shelter used temporarily when speed was a necessity and materials limited. The site was close to an emigrant camping place on Lodge Pole Creek, in use many years, one of the really pleasant stops where wood was plentiful and the water was clear and pure. Fat buffalo, antelope, and black-tailed deer were easy to get close to this favorite and well known emigrant camp.

Pine Bluffs tie and wood camp was set up by the contractors building that section of the railroad, and the activity there was more or less of the same pattern as many other camps that came before or after. Ox, mule and horse teams were used, as several hundred men worked to get out the ties. The pines

Sidney, Wyoming Territory, 1868

Pine Bluffs, Wyoming Territory, 1868

on the bluffs along the river, from which the town derived its name, soon disappeared before the axes of the woodchoppers.

The men in the camp were divided into factions, woodchoppers and teamsters. The wood was secured five to seven miles from Pine Bluffs camp and six-yoke ox teams could make the trip in one day. The horse and mule teams could move faster and so could haul from a greater distance. There were twenty of these six-yoke ox teams and thirty teams of four mules or horses. The wood cutting crews had always to be on the alert for Indians.

Wages in the camp were high, but to get out materials as fast as possible the bosses drove the choppers and teamsters and they drove the animals to the limit of their strength. The two factions at Pine Bluffs were constantly feuding, mostly because some of the bosses and their favorite teamsters were allowed to help themselves to whiskey at the camp store. Some of them consumed a tin-cupful before breakfast.

Men in such construction camps as this one appeared to be a uniformly hard lot, but actually they came from all walks of life and many only assumed a tough protective front. Tough or not, Photographer Hull found that, unless they were really fugitives from somewhere or something, they wanted pictures of their outfits. He was in camp long enough to watch the work and discovered how one of the sub-contractors used a common way of cheating called "cribbing." It consisted of piling the ties in a hollow square, topped over, and since they were measured in chords in the pile, the shortage was not easily detected.

Wyoming into Colorado

Although Hull had come part of the way from Chicago to Omaha by stagecoach, it was not much of a preparation for what he was to experience on the plains. By coach all the way from Omaha to Denver took six days and nights and the passengers slept bolt upright in their seats. No wonder he waited a few months until he could go part way by train.

At the end of the finished construction, the passengers were transferred from train to stagecoach. Several styles of coach were used, but the standard one, with boot both before and behind, had three seats inside to hold three passengers each. Seats on the Overland Stage Line were usually assigned by a system of first come, first served. The luckless individual who drew the middle section of the center seat was in for a miserable experience. The back of

that one was nothing but a broad leather strap that could be unhooked when not in use. Hull, with his eye for scenery, sat on top with the driver whenever possible.

From Fort Laramie in Wyoming Territory, to Denver, the stage route was the Territorial Road, following the old Cherokee trail part of the way. From Laramie it started up the Laramie River toward its source, then came out of the mountains and crossed the valley of the Cache la Poudre River. The valley was fringed with cottonwood trees and famous for its remarkable beauty in contrast to the open plains. There was a bridge over the Cache at one point and another across the Big Thompson near its junction with the Platte. These were toll bridges built by individuals in the earliest years of travel to the mountains, and the toll charges were five to eight dollars. Only when the water was dangerously deep for fording was it practical to pay such a high toll.

Hull photographed the cliff-like formations at the edge of the valley. Game was plentiful and the river full of trout. This was a favorite rest place where coach passengers might hunt or fish for an hour, if the Indians were quiet. They were loath to give up

Steamboat Buttes between Denver and Cheyenne

Cache la Poudre Valley

the valley to the white men and for a long time continued to run off the settlers' stock and to loot freight trains. Cabins were thick-walled with sod, with rifle loopholes.

During the long hours on the way to Denver, much of the talk among the stage passengers was of the gold strikes in the Clear Creek Mining towns which Hull planned to visit. With the Pikes Peak gold rush, dozens of mining camps appeared overnight in the mountains around Denver. Three on Clear Creek were booming since the discovery of gold there. Exciting things were taking place where a few years earlier hardly a white man had set foot. Central City and Black Hawk were only a mile apart, and Georgetown was twenty miles or so up the other branch of Clear Creek. Hull spent most of the next eight months in and around these three towns. It was a time full of events that made an important chapter in the history of Colorado.

A photographer with a load of equipment was fortunate to be able to get to Georgetown by stage in 1867. It had been such a short time since the first prospectors had picked their way through the trackless mountains on foot or on horseback. It was a day's trip from Denver to Georgetown, and the fare was five dollars up and four dollars down. During a feud between the stage lines, it was much higher. The daily stage went only as far as Central City. From there to Georgetown there was a toll road built by the mine owners and it was busy with ceaseless traffic. There were freight wagons, coaches, loads of hay on a five-day haul from the Cache la Poudre valley, prairie schooners, hand carts, log-haulers—every sort of vehicle.

Roads like this were a first necessity after the discovery of gold. Within the mining districts they were built by the members who owned the mines, who either donated the money or did the work. Larger capital was needed to build the roads leading from the districts to the plains trails, so companies were formed to build and operate them as toll roads. Toll charges were set for both vehicles and animals, and one of the early roads charged one and one-half cents a mile for a two-wheeled cart and three cents for a four-wheeled wagon. Oxen required a toll of three-fourths of a cent a mile and horses and mules, one cent.

Stagecoach near Steamboat Buttes

Douglas Mountain near Georgetown, Colorado, with stagecoach

Going up to Georgetown the scenery was very beautiful, and the changing view with patches of late snow on the mountains kept the attention of the passengers from the hazardous spots on the trail. An accomodating driver was willing to stop and rest his horses whenever Hull wanted to make photographs. Like all the stagecoach drivers, he had a store of tales to tell about the gold discoveries on Clear Creek.

Mining Towns

The first discovery at Georgetown was the Griffith Lode, located in 1859 by George Griffith. He, with his brother David, a pair of husky farmer boys from Kentucky, had aimed at the Central City locality to stake out mining claims, but when they arrived all the likely spots were taken. So the winter was spent learning about mines, growing beards, and generally wearing off the greenness. Then one lucky day George accidentally found the rich lode when he stopped to rest his horse on a hillside he had to climb to get around a beaver dam. The spot became the center of Georgetown.

The discovery of the Griffith lode brought the usual swarm of prospectors and followers to Georgetown and the resultant discovery of other deposits nearby. The Griffiths laid out the townsite and in partnership with one Cyrus Hiltebiddle built the toll road between Georgetown and Central City. In a few years Georgetown and Central City ranked with Denver as the three largest towns in Colorado Territory. But the real boom of Georgetown began when a silver deposit, the Belmont Lode, was discovered there in 1864

When Hull arived at Georgetown in 1867, a public ore market had just been established, J. C. Stewart had built the first reduction and smelting works. At the foot of the mountain was the Brown Company Reduction Works. The proprietors of both plants were eager to have photographs to send to doubters back East.

The silver boom having added to the excitement of the gold boom, Georgetown swarmed with miners and speculators, provisioners and panhandlers. The surrounding mountainsides were denuded of pine trees, cut down for logs to build the cabins that soon supplanted the first tents and leantos. When the town was surveyed and lots staked out, Elizabeth Griffith, the sister-in-law of the discoverer of the Griffith Lode, was given ten lots for being the first woman in camp, and one lot each was offered the next nine women.

61

Georgetown, Colorado, in 1867

Stewart's Reduction Works at Georgetown, Colorado, 1867

At a huge mass meeting in November 1867 the clamor for the county seat to be moved to Georgetown was so great that the Territorial Legislature was forced to call a special election which Georgetown won by an overwhelming number of votes. Young Hull watched it all, one of the first demonstrations of political maneuvering since he had left Omaha, and one of the experiences that spurred his interest in politics.

Life in Georgetown was an adventure in itself and Hull lingered and came back repeatedly after visits to Central City and Blackhawk. A fire swept through the town and another disaster that year was the Big Wind. The little Episcopal Church, the first church built in the town, was burned, rebuilt, and blown down in the "Big Wind of 67." Of that storm on the fifth of December, the Georgetown newspaper said:

> You might think that Georgetown, to all appearances sheltered in a little pocket in the hills and almost enclosed on three sides, would be proof against wind damage but unfortunately this is an illusion. When one

blast comes down Leavenworth Gulch and another down Argentine Gulch something has to give way when they meet in the middle of the town. The ones that came together yesterday blew down several buildings and unroofed many others, but you can't keep a good town down. We'll recover.

It seems there was a fortune-teller in Georgetown who had quite a clientele among the townspeople, so the news reporter went on to say:

> Madam Toughtale continues to enlighten the ignorant and superstitious ones of Georgetown on their future perigrinations, toils, pleasures and fortunes, nevertheless she failed to predict the "Big Wind."

The Barton House, in Georgetown, was declared by the *Rocky Mountain News* to be a hotel second to none in the Territory of Colorado. A young photographer had a chance to watch its debut in August, 1867, as a social center, on its way to become one of the most famous hotels in the West. In a few months the hotel register acquired the names of many well-known people, including famous actors and actresses,

Barton House at Georgetown

Mountains near Georgetown, Colorado Territory

millionaires, miners, great statesmen, governors, and French and English nobility. Over the years to follow, the register became a sort of record of the town's cultural development.

In May, 1868, General Grant, accompanied by Generals Sherman, Sheridan, and Dent, spent a week resting at the Barton House during Grant's political campaign. When the group came by stagecoach from Denver, Grant rode on the box beside Billy Updike, one of the most famous stage drivers of the time. Grant gave a speech from the balcony of the Barton House but a sudden shower came up and soaked the crowd and the speaker.

The Barton House stood on a knoll with a view of the valley. For the time and place it was a pretentious building, two and a half stories high, with a mansard roof and a small balcony over the entrance. Being a "three dollar hotel" it was considered "pretty fancy," as it was expressed then. Proprietor Billy Barton was an important personage and a popular host with a reputation as a judge of good food and wines.

Hull's picture is of the original Barton House, taken in the first year. Among the well-dressed group of guests, the men in hard-boiled shirts, the ladies in fashionable gowns, who were gathered on the steps to watch the stagecoach depart, there were probably some important personages, could they be identified. A few years after Hull made his photograph the hotel was partially destroyed by fire and rebuilt in practically the same style.

It was while young Hull was in the mining towns that he acquired a moustache and a goatee with the idea of appearing older. An editorial in the Georgetown newspaper may have furnished the impetus. The editor commented on the fact that mature men in Georgetown were almost invariably bearded, every style imaginable being acceptable as long as the basic ability to grow a crop of verdure was demonstrated. Until a young man showed ample acreage he was a fledgling. The same news writer said that the mark of a professional man semed to be that he trimmed his beard sometimes and drew his trousers down over his boots instead of stuffing them in the tops. When a Chinese laundryman was available, he wore a starched shirt with a paper collar and a black string tie.

Georgetown Silver Works at Georgetown

Black Hawk

In Black Hawk Hull made repeated visits to Professor Hill's reduction works, where he took photographs and watched the reduction process by which Hill saved the mining towns from economic disaster.

Hill had been a professor of chemistry at Brown University. A group of captalists brought him to Georgetown to work out a method of extracting silver from ore and reducing it to a concentrated form that would bear the cost of transportation to Swansea, Wales, for refinement.

After study and experimentation, part of it in Europe, Nathaniel P. Hill accomplished what he set out to do and in so doing brought the Clear Creek mining towns out of an economic slump, part of the general depression that spread over the whole country after the Civil War.

Hill was interesting to the photographer for his political views as well as for the way he handled silver ore, and when in later years Hill became United States Senator from Colorado, Hull followed his career as that of an old acquaintance.

Sid's Store at Black Hawk, Colorado Territory

Professor Hill's Works at Black Hawk

Blackhawk Company's Stamp Mill at Black Hawk

Central City

A month after gold was discovered on Clear Creek, there were five thousand people in the two settlements that became Central City and Black Hawk. Soon there were ten thousand, all in an area four miles square. Among the thousands of men, there were only five white women and seven squaws. Shelters were tents and leantos without furniture of any kind. Food was cooked on outdoor fires and provisions brought outrageous prices because of the difficulty of transportation into the mountains. The frenzied search for gold and dreams of fantastic wealth brought utter disregard for physical comfort.

It was in 1859 that gold was discovered by John Gregory at the site that became Central City. By the time Hull arrived in the district in 1867, the two settlements of Central City and Black Hawk had actually become one continuous town. The towns clung to the mountainsides, streets staggering along like crooked stairsteps, terrace above terrace, mine above mine, houses surrounded by the ugly stumps of the pine trees that once had made the gulch beautiful.

The rough life of the first years was difficult to outgrow. For a long time after the mineowners brought their families to the mining towns to live, there were several hundred men to every woman and women were not too safe on the streets even in the daytime. The writer's maternal grandmother, who was with her family in Black Hawk in the 60's, always more a small carved agate whistle on a ribbon around her neck. One shrill blast would have brought help from all sides. During this period a night watchman made the rounds every hour and called out the time and "All's well."

Arundel Hull made his photographs of Central City in 1867. It had settled down to a well-organized town. A group of busines men, confident that a narrowguage railroad would be built up the valley in a few years, were planning the Teller House and Opera House, famous today since the revival of Central City.

73

Gregory Point near Central City

Bobtail Lode near Central City, Colorado Territory

Even though the famous Opera House was not yet a reality in 1867, Central City had been having theatricals for a long time. There had been two seasons of regular theater on a circuit with Denver. Hull heard reminiscing of entertainments even before that time, especially of Madam Wakeley's troop of players. The plays were given on the second floor of a large log building and the audience was mostly booted, bearded, and six-shootered miners seated on wooden benches. The three Wakeley sisters who were loudly applauded for their acting, were openly scornful of the ineptitude of the rest of the cast who were any local males willing to blunder through the roles.

Seven churches were holding services in a variety of quarters in 1867 and 1868. It was invariably true, Hull found, that no matter how rough the atmosphere in the mining towns, one or two churches were among the first permanent buildings. All of his photographs of the early towns show their spires. While real churches were being put up, services were held in any available space; and in at least one case on Clear Creek, it was a room above a saloon. But since churches were respected by even the roughest characters regaling themselves in the lower room, silence was maintained during the service.

Two social groups were rather clearly defined in Central City in 1867. There were the business men and capitalists in the one, and the miners and other workmen in the other. The miners had unions and gymnastic clubs, and that year the Miner's and Mechanic's Institute was sponsoring the second season of bringing in lectures of high caliber. The Masons, Turners, and Odd Fellows contributed a great deal to the social life of the town. Their annual balls required tickets ranging from five to fifteen dollars each. On such occasions, after a midnight supper, dancing was resumed until daylight lessened the perils of the roads.

Both men and ladies dressed in the latest fashion. There was such a mania for organizing and joining that there was a meeting of some kind every night in the week. No wonder that young Hull lingered for nearly eight months on Clear Creek. Photography kept him in funds, and he found plenty of entertainment in the constantly shifting scenes of towns in the making.

Central City, 1868

Central City in 1868

Hull made frequent trips to the surrounding mountains to make photographs, and on one of these he had an experience that might have been near-tragedy. He had met a man who claimed to be experienced in photography, who offered to go along and help Hull while he made pictures where it was necessary to carry the equipment. The trip took several days, and although the stranger was a deafmute, he proved to understand photography and was indeed a help.

When Hull awoke one morning where the two had been sleeping in the open on a mountainside, he found his erstwhile friend had decamped in the night with Hull's camera and equipment—in fact everything except a frying pan and the blanket Hull was rolled in. After following him for two days, Hull caught up because he could travel so much faster than a man with a heavy load. Luckily such a black box of photographic material was noticed by everyone the thief chanced to encounter and was not hard to trace. Hull got back his valuable camera and supplies but seems never to have told his family what punishment he inflicted on the scoundrel. He was always suspicious that the man was not really a deafmute.

Mountain Towns and Views

Before going back to Denver after his stay in the mining towns on Clear Creek, Hull made a number of photographs in Boulder Canyon, a few of which he managed to preserve. The stage road down Boulder Creek forded and reforded the stream, and a new stage line on the route was using six-horse teams. It took a seasoned traveler to sit calmly when the driver let the horses out on the ever-curving trail, but the scenery was beautiful. Several stops were made while the passengers enjoyed their surroundings. Hull made photographs. A news item of that time described the contrast between the dark canyon and the snow-covered peaks as "sublime and beautiful in the extreme." Approaching Boulder, Hull was impressed by the beautiful setting of the little city, with tip-

tilted mountains forming a backdrop.

At Golden City, as it was called, snow covered the ground. Golden City shared the Clear Creek mining boom since it was situated on the creek where the valley widens. It already boasted several rather large brick buildings, and Hull found a friend of Omaha days was proprietor of Clark and Doolittle's store. Hull's picture shows it to be a classic of frontier period architecture and the men posed in front of it a study in tonsorial styles of the 1860's. Golden, on a direct route to the mines, grew so swiftly that at one time it rivaled Denver. *The Weekly Transcript* of Golden, in line with the custom of most early newspapers, often dealt in sarcasm and ridicule that seem childish but amusing from this distance. Rivalry between towns was keen. Typical was the item in the *Transcript* that year:

> Our Denver friends have a very uncomfortable time of it nowadays. They are nearly beside themselves with fear of losing their prospects of a branch railroad, and terribly shaken up with rumors of Indian depredations under their noses, and look pale at the vision of Cheyenne's future greatness. We

Boulder Canyon,　Colorado Territory

Boulder Canyon

Foothills (Flatirons) at Boulder, Colorado Territory

Clark and Doolittle, called Pete's Store, at Golden City

Golden, Colorado Territory

Golden, Colorado Territory, 1868

recommend to our eastern apothecaries to make a shipment of Mrs. Winslow's Soothing Syrup to Denver.

In 1868 Denver was seriously threatened by the Indian outbreak which ravaged most of eastern Colorado Territory. Happily the raiders did not come near the town, for it was practically without either arms or amunition and no doubt shaken up as the news item said. In October the townspeople were able to breathe more freely when a shipment of guns and military supplies arrived without being waylaid by the redskins.

Denver

Denver was started at the junction of Cherry Creek with the South Platte River when gold was discovered in the two streams. It was ten years old when Hull made his picture in 1868 with the South Platte bridge in the foreground. The town built up more closely to Clear Creek at first, and the stream was the first source of water for the settlers. Beside a small footbridge of cedar logs and rough planks, a flour barrel was sunk in the sand of the creek so that clear water could be dipped out of it with a bucket. Later the Larimer Street bridge was built close to the spot, and it was the scene of a Vigilante hanging which Hull photographed.

All the usual trials and tribulations that young settlements experienced, Denver had in full measure, including the special ones that were due to its isola-

tion. It was far beyond the outskirts of civilization with no backing at all for law enforcement. The dangers of travel across the prairies from the Missouri grew less and less as the railroad crept westward, but even after the rails reached Cheyenne, the nearest point to Denver, the trails from Cheyenne and Julesburg remained two perilous stretches. Hull luckily got to the mountains between periods of Indian troubles on the plains.

The gold found in Cherry Creek and the South Platte was dust washed down from deposits high in the mountains, but it was a different color, more nearly pure and much finer, than that found higher up. Ground as fine as flour from so much washing in the stream, a pinch of it would float in the air like a whiff of dust.

Most of the settlers and prospectors who came to Colorado Territory brought with them winter supplies and personal necessities but little money. Additional needs were obtained by barter. When the gold rush of 1859 brought swarms of people to the new towns, it also brought a new medium of exchange —gold nuggets and gold dust. Merchants and saloon keepers weighed out the gold on the counter and,

Denver in 1868

being human, gave themselves the advantage if possible. Everyone carried a bag or pouch of dust, to which the unscrupulous added a bit of brass filings.

The first bankers in the mountains were more in the nature of brokers. They exchanged coin for gold dust and nuggets and, using the Platte River dust as standard, paid from twelve to sixteen dollars an ounce. The gold was then shipped east for coinage. The cost and risk of transportation from the mining towns was great, and more problems arose as more and more mines were developed. Five per cent of the value of the shipment was charged against loss in transit and another five per cent of the value for express charges. The gold was in the hands of the broker from five weeks to three months, and a stagecoach sometimes carried $300,000 worth.

On July 20, 1860, the Clark Gruber Company began minting gold coins in the basement of their two-story brick building in the heart of Denver. It was the first banking firm to coin money in the mining area, and became and remained for many years the most trusted financial establishment in Denver. The first coins the company made were so soft they wore out

fast. The second year, when more alloy was added, they were still higher in the per cent of gold than the United States coins.

The coinage of money in Denver was without doubt a great advantage for both the mining companies and the people, but there grew a feeling that the percentage asked by the brokers was excessive. Public sentiment brought about a mass meeting of citizens who asked for the purchase of the Clark Gruber Mint by the United States government. In 1863 the building with all equipment was purchased by the United States for $25,000. The building was then enlarged as it appears in Hull's picture of 1867. The original building was left in the corner, a new part built around it, the front remodeled, and a flag pole added.

One of several schools for young ladies or young gentlemen, built by the Episcopal Church in Colorado Territory, was Wolfe Hall in Denver. Hull took his photograph the year it was built, 1867. It was located on the outskirts of town at the southwest corner of Seventeenth Street and Champa. During its long life as a finishing school for young ladies, it was enlarged, moved to another site, and enlarged again.

United States Branch Mint at Denver

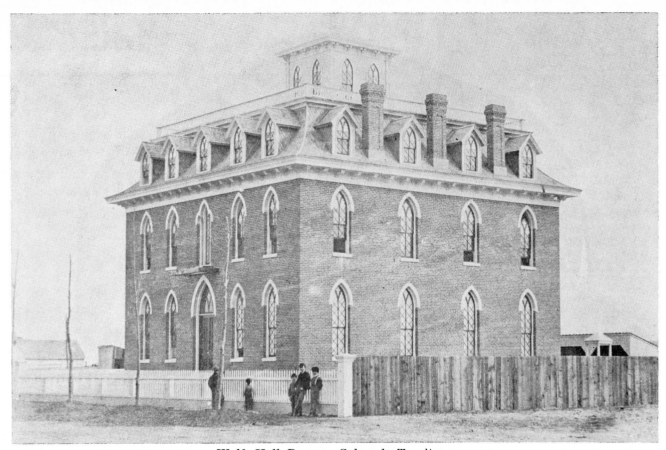

Wolfe Hall, Denver, Colorado Territory

Wyoming Territory

Hull left Denver temporarily to go by stagecoach to Salt Lake City. The album which contained samples of pictures he took on this trip was stolen when family household goods were stored. On the return trip he found the town of Green River had sprung up in Wyoming Territory, ready and waiting for the coming of the railroad. The site of the town had long been famous as an Overland Trail stop, stage and trading station, located a little to the south of the river fording. For a long time the Mormons maintained a ferry there because much of the year the river was deep. The toll over was from ten dollars up, and no one used the ferry if it could possibly be avoided. Before the coming of the railroad boomed the town, it was a dobie settlement on the flat, directly in front of the gorge through which the track was finally laid.

Green River had stormy beginnings and only a brief glory as a railroad terminus. The original group of settlers were firm in their belief that it would become a great city. There were two thousand people in a few weeks, confident that the town would be the winter terminus of the road, but the railroad company built a bridge and went on with its throng of followers. Green River continued to be interesting to travelers and emigrants for many years. The trout so easily caught in water colored green by the shale on the bottom, were a welcome change from the usual fare, and one did not need to be a geologist to appreciate the strange fossil formations, the agates and petrified woods, thickly strewn along Green River and Bitter Creek.

Some of the signs on the business buildings in Green River were familiar ones that had appeared in every terminus since Omaha. Among the men grouped in Hull's street scene in Green River was the notorious Jack Morrow, who seemed always to place himself in the center of things, and whose famous diamond shirt stud can be seen in the photograph.

The Overland Trail followed up Bitter Creek, and this was considered by the emigrants one of the most

Street view in Green River, Wyoming Territory. Signs on buildings read: Dixon and Grimes, Adams and Glover, Dr. Furley's Office, M. H. Barnett, J. A. Ware Co., California Clothing Co., T. A. Kent and Co.

Buttes on Bitter Creek, Wyoming Territory

Picnic Rock near Black Buttes, stage passengers posing

scenic parts of the trail. The valley was lined with towering rock formations. Along Rock Creek queer outcroppings also lined the stream. Bitter Creek was strongly alkali where the trail followed it, but ten miles higher up was clear and full of trout. All this territory had been found to be underlaid with lignite coal and some mines were already working in anticipation of the railroad furnishing an outlet for the product.

At Picnic Rock the stage passengers alighted and posed while Hull made a photograph. Black Buttes and Bitter Creek both were telepraph and stage stations and although this stretch of the Overland Trail was one of the most scenic, it was also one of the hardest to travel because of the heavy sand and alkali.

The wildest town Hull was to see in the West was Benton, Wyoming Territory. The rails reached a barren spot on the prairie in July, 1869, and in two weeks there were in the town of Benton three thousand people. As the business terminus of the railroad, Benton had all the characteristics in its short life, in an exagerated form. At one time the population reached five thousand, with rough characters and outlaws making up the majority.

All the daylight hours the streets were thronged with people. A young photographer from Indiana watched the crowd with interest—a motley crew of peddlers, miners, gamblers, Indians, Mexicans, Chinamen, railroad workers, bullwhackers, mule-skinners, capitalists, cappers, ministers, and prospectors. The fine alkali dust was six inches deep in the streets and the wind was unceasing. An eastern dandy who stepped off the train in a black broadcloth suit soon looked as if he had crawled out of a flour barrel. There was not a blade of grass or a growing thing in sight, but there were twenty-three saloons and five dance halls. The greatest institution of them all was a frame structure forty by one hundred feet, covered with canvas and floored for dancing, but serving as well for gambling. It was called "The Big Tent" and it had stood by turn in Julesburg, Cheyenne, and Laramie. Many a wild incident took place under its canvas roof.

Water had to be hauled to Benton from the Platte River and sold for ten cents a bucket or one dollar a barrel. A frequent comment was that tanglefoot

97

Benton, Wyoming Territory — the town that grew in a day and vanished in a night,
but it was red hot while it lasted

First engine on the Union Pacafic, with crew and onlookers. This was the workengine, actually the first engine.
The pictures that have been published as the first engine were of the first train carrying passengers

whiskey was cheaper and lasted longer. One or two deaths by violence a day was the customary average and law enforcement almost non-existent, although in short time Benton had a mayor, public health ordnances, and a newspaper.

Because Benton was the end of freight and passenger travel, twice a day immense trainloads of freight and humans arrived from the east and all the goods had to be unloaded, then reloaded on freightwagons for reshipment to more distant points. Daily stagecoaches took the passengers on westward.

Hull found old friends and acquaintances established in business in Benton. Gallagher and Megeath, which was the beginning of the firm of Paxton and Gallagher, wholesale grocers, had set up for business as they had at other points as the railroad progressed. A. H. Huyett, a wholesale and retail outfitter, had also put up his familiar sign. One of the canvas-covered frame buildings was shared by the Omaha J. A. Ware and Company Bank and T. A. Kent, Wines and Liquors. These two outfits shared a building in other terminal points, also, and between them probably saw a big share of the construction payroll.

On August 11, 1868, General Grant was at Benton during his political campaign, and Hull saw him for the second time, no doubt making photographs which have long since disappeared. Grant was accompanied by Buffalo Bill, who stood on a drygoods box on a street corner and thanked the crowd in Grant's behalf for the hearty reception given the Commander-in-Chief. Then Buffalo Bill produced an old watch and said the General had asked him to auction it off to defray his expenses. After the watch was sold, Grant gave a brief speech which the editor of the newspaper treated very sarcastically.

One of the incidents Hull liked to tell about in later years took place in Benton. At the request of his friend from Omaha who was in charge of the Ware Company Bank, he spent several nights with him in the boarded-up canvas tent. Equipped with guns and amunition the two waited in vain for an expected hold-up of which the banker had been tipped off. If the warning was authentic, the outlaw must have decided two men were more than he wanted to handle and after several more or less sleepless nights the tension eased.

Another incident of his stay in Benton was photo-

Street scene, Benton, Wyoming Territory. Stores of Gallager and Megeath,
A. H. Huyett, T. A. Kent, A. J. Ware and Co.

Jack Morrow at Benton. Morrow seated on barrel surrounded by thirteen other men.

graphing the notorious Jack Morrow. The picture Hull saved for himself shows this frontier character seated on a barrel, surrounded by a group of men. That he had the center of the stage was true to his character. No doubt some of the other men in the picture were notorious, too, in one way or another, but were so overshadowed by Morrow that Hull merely wrote on the picture—Jack Morrow at Benton.

Jack Morrow

Morrow started his career on the Plains as a common thief but his activities, as he became older, carried him into the upper brackets of swindling.

There seems to be no record of him before he appeared on the Plains in the late 1850's but he was well known through Nebraska and Wyoming Territories and around Denver, long before the coming of the railroad. In a few years his eccentric ways of wasting money and his stupendous drunken sprees became legend from Omaha to the mountains and the mining towns. Then, after he had killed a man in a gun fight, his reputation as a bad man was established.

Jack Morrow's career on the Plains began as a government teamster hauling freight to the mountains. During many trips from Omaha to Denver or Salt Lake City, he worked at accumulating a stake by tapping his freights. This was the simple practice the term implies, stealing part of the load and caching it along the road to be picked up later. From the start of his route to the end of it, he soon became known as a braggart and a boaster but it was considered unwise to question his tall tales.

The enormous vanity of the man prompted one of his first acquisitions when he became prosperous. It was a huge diamond shirt stud which he wore constantly, regardless of how badly the shirt it was attached to needed laundering. He wore it high up near his collar where it would show above the high-buttoned coats that were in vogue in the 1860's. (It can be seen in Hull's pictures.)

Morrow worked at his teamster's job until he had enough capital to go into partnership with a Frenchman known on the Plains as Old Constant. He was Alex Constant, who had been, for many years, a fur trader on the Missouri River for The American Fur Company. At Doby Town on the Platte River near Fort Kearney, the two operated a trading post and made money in record time selling to the wagon trains and stage passengers on the Oregon and Overland

Trails.

Constant was a crafty old plainsman, experienced in the ways of the frontier if anybody was, but he was no match for the wily Morrow, who one day robbed his French partner and fled westward to the junction of the North and South Platte Rivers. There, in 1860, in an area already recognized as a grazing paradise, familiar to him from his many freighting trips, Jack Morrow established his famous Junction Ranch.

The ranchhouse proper at Junction Ranch became one of the sights of the trail, admired by the endless stream of weary emigrants and travelers whose wagons rolled westward through a perpetual ribbon of dust. Quite in contrast to the usual sod ranchhouse with a sod roof, it met the surprised eyes of the travelers, an imposing structure built entirely of cedar logs, roof and all. It was two and a half stories high and sixty feet long and stood on the open prairie south of the river fork, a few miles southeast of the site of the present city of North Platte, Nebraska.

This area around the junction of the rivers had long been known because of the trading posts at Cottonwood Springs and O'Fallon's Bluff. These two had served the thousands of people who had passed up the trails since 1858. The historically famous Box-elder Creek Mail and Pony Express Station was started near the junction in 1860, the year Morrow set up his ranch and trading post.

When emigrants began to meet with various misfortunes near Junction Ranch and tried to by-pass it, Morrow thwarted all such attempts and made sure every freight wagon and prairie schooner had to pass his layout. There were hills and canyons south of the ranch buildings. Taking advantage of his position between them and the river, he dug a wide and deep ditch across the natural route westward. He edged it with a high dike and it extended from the ranch buildings to the bank of the river, something like a half a mile. Thus did he insure his position for the plans he had. The ditch is still there today, half filled and sodded over, not looking so formidable. But it was a real barricade, too deep and too steep-banked for heavy ox or horse-drawn wagons to cross.

In due time word was passed back along the trails that Jack Morrow was stocking his ranch with the help of some "bad" Indians and renegade white men.

105

Morrow kept several hundred Sioux, with their squaws and papooses, in primitive comfort in a camp near the ranch. With them were some white squaw-men, Jack Sharp, Tod Randall, Bob Rowland, and a man named Turgeon. All the white men could speak the Sioux language. The whole camp was supplied with rations, liquor, and goods from Morrow's trading post. In return, the men obliged their benefactor by stampeding the stock of the emigrants and running off the herds.

The sheer bluffs and maze of deep-cut canyons along the river offered ideal temporary hideouts for any number of stolen cattle and horses and it was a risky business for the owners to go far from the trail in search of them. When they gave up hope and went on without their stock, the Indians rounded the animals up and drove them in with the fast growing herds on Morrow's sandhills range.

At one point the lofty bluffs on the south side of the Platte rise to a peak visible for many miles. The Sioux used it as a lookout and signal station and the white men knew it as Sioux Lookout. Today the figure of a Sioux Indian scout, sculptured of Indiana lime-stone, stands on the highest point where a view of the wide valley extends for miles east and west. In the 1860's Morrow's Sioux kept constant watch there, reporting to him the size and condition of every approaching wagon train long before it reached the ranch.

It became the custom of the emigrants to double and triple the guards on the herds at night when this section of the trail was reached, and to use every precaution against the stampede of their stock by Morrow's raiders. Even so, scarcely a wagon train passed without the loss of an animal or two, if not the whole herd. Soon the number of cattle and horses on the range of Junction Ranch outnumbered by hundreds the stock of the neighboring ranchers who depended on the laws of nature for their increase.

Morrow was always sympathetic, big-hearted, and overly generous in offering to sell replacements to the distressed losers of stock. The unwary were sometimes fooled by this move, which was not so much to unload animals previously stolen, as it was a trick to find out whether the emigrant had any sizeable amount of cash on him. Sometimes one of Morrow's henchmen offered to find the stampeded stock for a certain sum, another fake offer for under no conditions were the animals ever returned. But if, during the dickering, the owner was unwise enough to give any indication he had money, he was later waylaid and robbed on the trail.

The diverse enterprises Morrow developed from his strategically situated ranch rapidly made him a rich man, and the Morrow law of intimidation prevailed over a wide territory. Legitimate sales of provisions and articles necessary to travelers on the Oregon and Overland Trails brought the high prices he had no scruples about asking. Furs and buffalo robes, secured by barter from the Indians, and buffalo meat and beef, he stored in great quantities. Once a year he hauled it all down to Omaha. It was a profitable business but it also gave the swaggering braggart an opportunity to put on a grand show with his long, impressive caravan of freight wagons, piled high.

Perhaps the easiest source of revenue for Jack was a stand of cedar trees in Moran Canyon near his ranch. Besides cutting all he wanted for his own use, he sold quantities for telegraph poles, two thousand to a contract. It mattered not that the land where the cedars grew was not his; threats were sufficient to keep anyone else from cutting logs there. Because of his hold over the Indians, they did not attack his woodcutters as they did other outfits.

During his years as a freight teamster, Morrow had learned all the possibilities of the country between Omaha and Denver and Salt Lake City. When his ranch was well established, his field of operation widened over much of this area. One of the first to recognize the ease with which lignite coal could be mined in the surface deposits in Wyoming Territory, he had a coal mine operating near Black Buttes at least a year before the railroad reached there.

As the Union Pacific construction approached, Morrow already knew where the good stands of timber were and he secured contracts for hundreds of thousands of feet of cord wood and railroad ties. The Cheyenne and Laramie newspapers and *The Frontier Index* carried his ads for woodcutters and for ties to be delivered at the track. Later he deliberately boasted of short-counting and overcharging on these contracts. A practice called "cribbing," which consisted of arranging ties or cordwood in piles with a hollow center, was a common way of cheating.

Another of Morrow's enterprises was a mule freight train operating between Laramie and Salt Lake City. As all these activities gave him the opportunity to swindle on contracts and freight shipments, more of his time and interest centered on them rather than harrassing the emigrants. He also lost some of his hold over his Indian factotems, and the ranch, now well stocked, was left more and more to the care of his foreman, Hewey Morgan. Morgan seemingly never did wholly approve of stealing from the emigrants, although his aversion to the practice was not strong enough to make him give up a well paid job. He was Morrow's righthand man for many years.

Hewey Morgan was a versatile and capable foreman, who was also bookkeeper and salesman for Junction Ranch and for Jack Morrow's other interests as well. Some contemporaries thought he was a partner in Morrow's enterprises. At any rate he took over the responsibility for everything when Morrow was in his frequent drunken spells and must have performed his duties well, for Jack put unlimited trust in him.

Eugene Ware, commander of the military post at

Fort McPherson, some fifteen miles from Junction Ranch, in relating his experiences there in his book, *The Indian Wars of 1864,* tells of being a guest of Jack Morrow and Hewey Morgan at the ranch. He and the other officers of the post were invited to dinner. Tincups were kept filled with champagne before and during a meal of broiled antelope heart, baked buffalo humps, and fried beaver tails. Entertainment was furnished by a young gentleman from a neighboring ranch who could recite poetry and do impersonations. He was probably a squawman for he had been given an Indian name by the Sioux, but Ware told of encountering him years later in Ohio, where he was a prominent minister.

The army officers from McPherson were suspicious that their invitation had not been purely social. Comparing notes afterward, they found that each of them had been asked privately, by either Morrow or Morgan, to use his influence in securing Morrow a contract from the government to supply the fort a large amount of shelled corn at a ridiculously high price.

The layout at Junction Ranch grew to include a row of "Pilgrim's quarters." These were sleeping huts which were rented to overnight stoppers, and the third story of the ranchhouse was also used for this purpose. Pilgrim was the half scornful name applied to the newcomer to the Plains, just as back East he would have been called a Greenhorn and farther west he would become a Tenderfoot. No Pilgrim could be fastidious about a place to sleep. Although the upper floor of the ranchhouse was divided into rooms, the cross logs had not been sawed out for doors. So, going from one room to another necessitated crawling over six feet of cedar log wall. Yet these rooms were usually occupied at a high price by travelers who needed to get out of the weather. Because of Morrow's devious ways of doing business, quarrels and arguments with Pilgrims, wagon bosses, and stage passengers were everyday occurrences.

There came a time, however, when Junction Ranch was an asset to the neighboring settlers. When the Sioux Indians were drawn into the Cheyenne War in 1864, numbers of ranches in the Platte valley were looted and burned and some white people were killed. Because the Morrow ranchhouse was so large and substantially built, the neighboring ranchers gathered there and fortified it with sod walls. Two things prob-ably account for the fact that the Indians did not attack it, Morrow's close association with several hundred Sioux who considered him their benefactor, and his status as a squawman. Consequently, for a long time during the Indian trouble, Junction Ranch held open the line of communication along the Platte.

After some years, Morrow's squaw wife died and he married a white woman. Nothing was ever known of her except that an occasional visitor to the ranch said that she was refined, modest, neatly dressed, and seemed rather out of place. So far as is known, Morrow had no children, never having acknowledged any to his associates or neighbors.

It isn't possible that other ranchers on the Platte were blind to what an unscrupulous character Morrow was. They were no doubt desirous of getting along peaceably, appreciative of his protection during the Indian troubles and perhaps humanly influenced by his wealth, for on election day in September, 1866, he was made one of the three County Commissioners of Lincoln County, Nebraska Territory. By then his persecution of the emigrants had perhaps stopped entirely, as his other interests had become more important to him.

Arundel C. Hull, the young photographer who made the pictures of Jack Morrow at Benton and Green River in Wyoming Territory, little dreamed that six years later he would marry a girl whose father had been a victim of Morrow's thievery. The experience of the Alanson Miller family was typical of what many emigrants suffered at his hands. Traveling from Wisconsin to Colorado in what the daughters of the family described in letters to the folks back home as "the finest and best outfitted prairie schooners we have seen on the trail," the wagon train included a herd of horses driven by the Miller sons, to stock a ranch in Colorado. The herd was stampeded by Morrow's men between Junction Ranch and O'Fallon's Bluffs and a fake offer to find them was refused. Among several fine horses in the herd was a thoroughbred named Rob Roy. The writer is intrigued with the idea that Rob Roy might have been the horse on which Morrow was said to look like a model cavalier.

When he retired from his ranch in the late 1860's, Morrow lived in Omaha in a luxurious home and

concentrated on government contracts and general speculation. His brazen arrogance never failed him and his wealth continued to increase through his contracts and the poker games he played with visiting Congressmen. He bragged about his contract swindles as he had the scurvy tricks of his early years, but the incident he delighted most to recall was the poker game in which he won sixty thousand dollars from the members of a committee sent out from Washington to investigate irregularities in government contracts.

In the 1860's Omaha still tolerated open gambling, requiring only the occasional payment of light fines. The two most popular gambling places were on the second floor of the Pioneer Block on Farnam Street between Eleventh and Twelfth, in the business district.

One of these was run by a character appropriately called Stuttering Brown. All of Brown's customers did not leave his gambling room happy, and someone took revenge on him by shooting him from ambush as he rode in a stagecoach bound for the Black Hills.

The other gambling room was equipped with a dumb waiter between it and a pawn shop on the first floor. The proprietor, Dan Allen, furnished this convenience to those of his patrons who ran out of cash, and at the same time avoided the obligation of some I O U's. Many a faro player literally lost his shirt as well as his money and valuables playing in Dan Allen's gambling room, and of course the pawnbroker made a fortune.

Jack Morrow became a frequent customer of these establishments back in the days when he was driving freights out of Omaha. In his more affluent years, after he had moved to Omaha to live, he was still more familiar there. He also became an habitue of the genteel and plushly elegant gambling room of Matt Harris on the second floor of the Central Block. It was between Twelfth and Thirteenth Streets on Douglas, only a few blocks over from the Brown and Allen rooms; but it was the resort of "high-toned" players, the more prosperous citizens with social standing and a number of gay army officers. Morrow was recognized even in this gentlemanly environment as a tough citizen and a bad man with a gun. There is a story of a scene he created in the plush Harris place when he was on one of his frequent sprees.

After he had lost three thousand dollars, Morrow whipped out his six-shooter and accused the dealer of cheating. He demanded his money back or he would put a bullet through the dealer. In his befuddled state he failed to realize the dealer was the proprietor himself. Harris quietly counted out the money and after Morrow had pocketed it, invited him to have a drink before he left. Morrow accepted, but, after ordering the drinks, Harris stepped into the next room and suddenly reappeared with two revolvers in his hands saying, "Jack, you had the drop on me, but now I have it on you. Put the money and your gun on the table and if you make any attempt at gunplay I will kill you or one of my men will."

Thus out-maneuvered the red-faced Morrow burst into a loud guffaw, declaring that he had only been joking anyway, but he did as he was ordered. Harris replied that he wasn't sure it was a joke until he had his own guns in his hands. Jack took his drink and departed with a suggestion from Harris that he come around next day when he was sober to get his gun.

Perhaps it was such incidents as this that made some of Jack Morrow's contemporaries doubt his courage. Although it is true that he killed a man

111

named Murphy in a gun battle during his early years on the plains, it seems to be the only killing he was directly responsible for. One such incident was enough to establish his reputation as a killer. The bad whites and Indians he kept under obligation did many a nefarious chore for him. His arrogance and bullying needed only their backing.

Luxurious living meant only more time spent in dissipation for Jack Morrow. In a few years his gambling and drinking began to consume his wealth faster than he could replace it, and the shirts on which the enormous diamond shone began to look soiled again. Prolonged debauches finally undermined the rugged constitution that had survived so many years of abuse, and in 1885 the erstwhile dapper, notorius thief and swindler died in poverty.

The reason Morrow was at Benton at the time of the photograph, and not at his headquarters ranch at the junction of the Plattes, was that he owned a coal mine at Black Buttes, west of Benton, which was then in operation. Morrow was also under contract to furnish ties for the railroad and advertised in *The Frontier Index* for 25,000 cords of wood to be cut be-

tween Green River and Black Buttes. And he was operating a mule freight train between Laramie and Salt Lake City. These activities made him a frequent traveler to the end of the railroad.

In the language of the times, Benton was a red hot town while it lasted. But when the terminus moved on, in a matter of hours everything in it was loaded on flat cars and the most notorious Hell-on-Wheels of the railroad construction days disappeared as if it had never been. In a brief time not even the five score graves on Boot Hill could be distinguished.

One of the many forts the Government established throughout the territories in an attempt to keep the Indians under control while the railroad was being built, and protect the settlers and travelers, was Fort Steele. It was toward the headwaters of the North Platte River in Wyoming Territory, and was established June 30, 1868, by Colonel R. I. Dodge, at what was considered a strategic point in case of Indian troubles.

The soldiers were quartered in tents while permanent log barracks were being built. The framework of some of these buildings was being put up when Hull took his photographs of Fort Steele. The

Cottonwood trees at Fort Steele

Bridge across North Platte at Fort Steele

Fort Steele, Wyoming Territory, 1868

Platte River was a clear, cold stream here, edged with cottonwood trees. The fort was situated in the center of an Indian hunting and trapping area. With the soldiers for protection, the white men took over and the fort became a rendezvous for ranchmen, hunters, and trappers.

It was necessary for the railroad to cross the Platte at Fort Steele. The presence of the Fort prevented building of a settlement at the crossing, so the migrant roughs, awaiting the coming of the road, had to set up their tents on the alkali flat two or three miles west. This was Brownsville, and in twenty-four hours five hundred hangers-on, some of whom had been invited to leave their last stop, had come to squat. In June, 1868, a Pony Express was started from Laramie City to Brownsville.

Before the railroad reached the area, the only things to be feared were the Indians. But with Brownsville came a class of white men quite as dangerous as the red ones. Along with more serious crimes, they stole anything they could get their hands on, including horses and mules almost within sight of the fort. Since the need for some control of the

roughs at Brownsville was urgent, the Vigilantes of Cheyenne, though a hundred fifty miles away, considered it within their field of activity. But the need was not long. Brownville was only a brief stopover for the outlaws on their migration from Cheyenne to Benton.

While Benton and Brownsville were flourishing, the road building crews were pressing on with all speed possible across the desert-like country toward Green River, a stretch that brought discouraging misery to the emigrant trains. The graders, bridge-builders, and track layers worked through the twenty-four hours completing five miles of road a day across the Great Divide to Black Buttes, mostly in and on rock. When this, one of the most difficult accomplishments of the building of the railroad, was over and Green River had been passed, it was the end of the terminus towns—the "Moving Towns" or the "Hell-on-Wheels" as they were commonly called. The swarm of lawless drifters that had originated at Fort Kearney in Nebraska, and had followed the rails for eight hundred and fifty miles, disintegrated and took themselves off to new and less congested bases of activity.

Laramie—Vigilantes

From Benton and Fort Steele, Hull continued east as far as Cheyenne, traveling by train over the same route he had come by stagecoach a year and a half before. Where a great empty plain had spread out in a magnificent panorama, there now stood the town Laramie. The settlers had recognized the plain as a wonderful grazing country and the surrounding mountains were known to be rich in minerals. The streams were full of trout and wild game was abundant. Emigrants had long been taking the opportunity to supplement their provisions when they crossed this area. All this and the beautiful scenery gave Laramie *City* excellent prospects in the eyes of the settlers, who dubbed it "The Gem City of the Mountains."

When Hull came in October, 1868, the town was five months old. The railroad had reached the site on May 9th and the next day the first freight train discharged its cargo. It was a huge load of freight, human and otherwise, the cars piled high with iron rails, ploughs, scrapers, tents, 7x9 shanties, lumber, groceries, peddlers and their packs, stoves, boxes of crockery, baskets of tinware, barrels of liquor, knocked-down wooden shacks, boxes, bales and bundles of household goods, with men, women, and children perched on top. The terminus had moved to Laramie.

There had been such strife over town lots in Cheyenne, and so much money made by speculators, that every man in the country having the price of a lot in Laramie was waiting for the opening. In less than two weeks something like five hundred buildings of various styles and materials were up. There were more saloons than other business places and almost as many dance halls and gambling dens. One dance hall was opened by a pious looking, but too avid gentleman who was sent out by a missionary society with six hundred dollars with which to start a mission.

In three months there were five thousand people in Laramie, and probably a fifth of them were undesire-

Laramie, Wyoming Territory, 1868

ables. The town was destined to endure in its turn the same human driftwood that had briefly populated North Platte, Julesburg, and Cheyenne. There were respectable people in Laramie who had come to settle permanently and conduct legitimate business. They did so under such difficulties they were finally impelled to take the enforcement of the law into their own hands.

A Vigilante Committee was formed, although it only drew the interest of twenty men. By August conditions had become so serious that the committee decided it was time to begin work. Their first arrest and hanging was a young man called "The Kid" who, unfortunately, was not a leader and would have been glad to leave town. As a result of this ill-advised incident, the rough element organized and held a number of meetings developing plans to outwit the Vigilantes. Gaining strength in numbers, the outlaws practically took over the town. There were so many crimes committed that the citizens became aroused to a high pitch and a second Vigilante Committee of somewhere between four and five hundred men was the result.

At a meeting in the railroad roundhouse, plans were made in deliberate fashion for raids on several dens of infamy. On the night of October 18, 1868, the committee met on the west side of the railroad tracks, all heavily armed. Members were assigned to squads under the leadership of a Civil War veteran, Thomas B. Sears. Most of the men were, like Sears, highly respected townsmen sincerely interested in an orderly and well-governed town in which to spend the rest of their lives. Many of them became in later years Laramie's most valued citizens.

Men were posted at the railroad crossings and at all the roads leading out of town, all precaution being taken to keep their movements secret. The first visit was made to the Belle of the West Dance House. It was brightly lighted and full of dancers, gaudily and fashionably dressed women, gamblers and outlaws. Deputy Sheriff Charlie Ames guessed that something was afoot and passed among the Vigilantes warning them to keep the peace. His arms were suddenly pinned to his sides and he was escorted outside just in time, for, as the fiddler struck up the first notes of "Money Musk," a shot rang out.

This shot was supposed to be a signal for simul-

Dance house; Keystone Hall, at Laramie

Railroad shops at Laramie

taneous action by all the squads, but someone had become excited and had fired it prematurely. At the sound, Ace Moore drew his gun and fired into the Vigilantes. Con Wagner followed his lead. Pandemonium broke loose. For fifteen minutes the two outlaws and their followers exchanged shots with the Vigilantes, while women wailed and men cursed. In a cloud of smoke the outlaws were finally overpowered. Wagner and Moore were full of bullets but were not dead so they were hustled out and hanged beside a log stockade. One of the musicians was killed in the fracus, also one of the Vigilantes and another outlaw, and about fifteen others more or less seriously wounded.

While one squad of Vigilantes was busy with Wagner and Moore, another squad had surrounded a house near a saloon where a notorious character called Big Ned was known to be asleep. When the search party entered the room, Big Ned was not in the bed but under it. He was dragged out and hanged beside Wagner and Moore. The three bodies were left dangling until the next day so that all fellow outlaws could profit by the sight. This was fortunate for

122

young photographer Hull who just happened to be in Laramie. He was ready with his camera as soon as the light was good. He had been alerted the night before when a hotel clerk had remarked that the Vigilantes must be up to something because the whole town was so quiet. Soon the noise of the gunfight proved him right.

After Moore, Wagner, and Big Ned had been taken care of, the Vigilantes captured another desperate character, Steve Young, known as Big Steve. A substantial citizen had interceded for him and he was released on condition that he would leave town and not return. He did leave and went as far as Fort Sanders but came back early the next morning, October 19, 1868. He was of course seen by a Vigilante and the Committee captured him once more and hanged him to a telegraph pole without ceremony. It was close to the railroad station near where South B. Street crossed the tracks. He too was left hanging until daylight and Hull got a photograph.

After four of their kind had paid the penalty for their misdeeds, most of the roughs left Laramie without waiting for railroad accomodations and the Vigilantes returned to their own pursuits. The triple

Outlaws hanged at Laramie. Con Wagner, Ace Moore, Big Ned,
beside what appears to be a log stockade

Steve Young, hanged at Laramie by vigilantes

hanging was called "judicious." Laramie's house-cleaning by her citizens was typical of the extreme measures necessary to cope with conditions in many of the new settlements. A necessary evil, the Vigilantes ceased to exist as soon as the need for them was past.

Feeling lucky to be in Laramie at the time of such goings-on, Hull included in his photographs one of the roundhouse where the Vigilantes met to make their plans, and one of the Freund Gun Store, which supplied guns and ammunition to Vigilantes and outlaws impartially.

The Freunds were an interesting pair of brothers, Frank and George, who were born in Germany and came to the United States when Frank was twenty. George was several years younger. Frank had worked at the family trade of gunmaking in London, Paris, and Vienna before the two boys came to America. He served in the Union Army during the Civil War and after its close the brothers worked as gunsmiths along the Union Pacific, following the progress of its construction.

In 1867 the Freunds opened a shop in Cheyenne. They were both skilled craftsmen and also inventors.

Frank acquired eighteen patents in his name and George, three. A short time after opening their first shop in Cheyenne they became dealers in guns, ammunition, and hunting supplies, beside their regular work of making, altering, and repairing guns.

The Freunds set up a second store at Laramie and temporary ones at Benton and Green River in Wyoming Territory, and at Bear River and Corrine in Utah Territory. They made their ammunition at an out-of-the-way place on Powder River, away from the settlements, where they built a dugout and a dutch oven for melting lead and tin for shot. Buffalo fat fires under and on top of the oven created heat enough to melt the metals.

After the completion of the railroad, the Freunds moved all their business to Denver, where they had a fine big establishment. But when the slaughter of the buffalo was going strong in 1875 they sold out and went back to Cheyenne where they made the Freund-Improved Sharps, a favorite with the buffalo hunters.

It is unfortunate that the names of the men in Arundel Hull's photograph of the Freund Brother's shop in Laramie are not known. Quite obviously

Freund Gun Store, Laramie. The store of famous gunsmith. A dozen men in front of store, deer hanging, another deer behind saddle of horseman

some of them are important characters. The central figure might well be one of the Freunds since he has the appearance of posing in front of his establishment. In 1869 Hull was in Corrine, Utah Territory, for the second time, and then in the company of William H. Jackson. There they made a photograph showing the Freund Brothers large, wooden, gun-shaped sign on their temporary quarters shared with a jeweler.

Dale Creek

Between Laramie and Dale Creek much of the railroad construction was through solid rock. That was only one of many difficulties encountered. When General Dodge accidentally discovered a route that greatly simplified the problem of getting a railroad over the great divide, there was another obstacle yet to be whipped. That was the building of a bridge across the deep canyon formed by Dale Creek, just west of Sherman, the highest point on the whole road.

By agreeing to give some prints to the engineer and work boss, Hull was given a ride on the work engine so he could take photographs of the Dale Creek Bridge. He made two excellent pictures, one with the first engine and the work crew on the bridge.

This railroad bridge over Dale Creek became fa-

128

mous while it was being built as one of the wonders of the whole continental route. It was completed in June, 1868, built entirely of timber trestles. This was especially remarkable because it was 136 feet high and 650 feet long. It spanned the deep ravine of a creek which flows into the Cache la Poudre River. The Denver branch of the Overland Trail passed near the bridgesite, crossed the creek near it, and followed up Dale Creek and the Poudre until it reached the headwaters of the Laramie River.

The original Dale Creek bridge of Hull's photographs was followed nine years later by a second remarkable feat when, during the whole process of replacing the wooden structure with an iron one, no train was delayed more than twenty minutes.

During the building of the original bridge there were two towns near. The construction workers camp of five hundred men and their families was a well-organized little village laid out with streets. But three miles away was a very different sort of camp called Dale City, with forty-five pine log buildings "very branchily laid," ranging in size from 12x14 to 30x40. Four of the larger ones were dance halls and one a court room. There were three hotels which

Dale Creek bridge with first Union Pacific engine

Dale Creek Bridge

one visitor said were run on the burrowing system because it was necessary to learn the sleeping habits of a gopher before one could comfortably sleep in them. Life in Dale City was perilous and a cemetery was needed from the very start.

The work engine took Hull two miles east of the bridge to the top of Sherman Hill. Sherman Station on a plateau was the highest point on the railroad and a spot where all travelers liked to get off the train and look about at the unique rock formations and huge boulders. Hull photographed some of them, including one called the Hen's Nest.

Hen's Nest at Sherman, Wyoming Territory

Cheyenne

When Hull crossed Wyoming Territory going west in 1866, there was nothing but open prairie where Cheyenne stood when he returned late in 1868. The railroad had reached the site on November 13, 1867, and by the following spring more than three hundred business enterprises were in operation. The first freight train to roll into Cheyenne brought everything movable from Julesburg, including a horde of questionable characters who were no asset. In a year, the population increased to six thousand, the town had earned the name "Magic City of the Plains."

Outlaws began their activities as soon as the settlers arrived. Robberies, shooting scrapes, and trouble with landjumpers were everyday occurrences. Since the townsite was on the railroad grant, the railroad company had the authority, when conditions became too hectic, to call for the soldiers stationed at nearby Fort Russell. The soldiers ran the whole populace out of town and held them three miles south of the townsite until they promised to respect the law.

With the constant shifting of a large proportion of the people, conditions soon became intolerable again, and the permanent settlers followed the pattern of other frontier towns and organized a Vigilante Committee. It functioned with good results. Although the methods of the Vigilantes seldom called for a jail, Cheyenne maintained one in 1868, a 20x20 tent. One night two visitors, adventurous and prominent citizens of Denver, became so convivial and noisy they were put in it for the night. Early in the morning they realized their plight and decided the best way to save face was to turn their incarceration into a joke. Before daylight they moved the tent and set it up on the bank of Crow Creek. When the marshal found it there a mile east of town, the two prisoners sat with a bucket of water and a tin cup, explaining that they were thirsty and didn't want to be accused of breaking jail.

Two incidents of Cheyenne's beginning show how

133

Street view in Cheyenne, Wyoming Territory, 1868

opposing forces struggled in the development of the early settlements. A group of people in Cheyenne thought the infant city should show its sophistication by staging a prize fight. It was put on in a makeshift ring for $500 a side and lasted one hour and forty-three minutes for 126 rounds, ending in a foul. While the fight was going on another group of citizens was meeting to make arrangements for opening the first school in Cheyenne, which also turned out to be the first one in Wyoming Territory.

Cheyenne was a year old when Hull made his photograph. The Rocky Mountain Star Printing House published a daily and a weekly newspaper beginning December 8, 1867. Two other newspapers started up that year also, *The Daily Leader* in September, and the *Daily Argus* in October. The Omaha firm of Gallagher and Megeath had one of their wholesale and retail stores a few doors beyond the *Star* printing plant. In addition to having these stores at the railroad terminal points, this company did an enormous business as a commission and forwarding company. They handled 90% of the Union Pacific freight that went on from the end of construction. The goods were transferred to freight wagons and hauled to all points up to the connection with Central Pacific which was approaching from the west coast. Other freighting outfits also carried on a huge business from Cheyenne to Denver and the mining camps, requiring the use of hundreds of mule and ox trains.

The first murder committed in Cheyenne had a sequence in an incident in Denver later when Hull was there. In the vicinity of Cheyenne, at a place in the hills called Robber's Roost, a sixteen year old Irish boy, camp keeper for a construction crew, was murdered. Two men named Dugan and Howard were arrested, but Howard escaped. Dugan was tried but had so many friendly witnesses that he escaped paying the penalty, as he had escaped paying for a similar crime in Central City, Colorado Territory. Justice finally caught up with him in Denver.

Vigilantes—Denver

It was November, 1868, when Hull returned to Denver, again by stagecoach from Cheyenne. Soon after, one of the first Vigilante hangings in Denver occurred. The victim was Sam Dugan who had escaped from a posse at Laramie and had gone unpunished for murders committed at Cheyenne and Central City. The man was even then not hanged for murder but for robbery. The event took place on December 1, 1868, and once more Hull was able to get a photograph before the victim was cut down.

It was late in the evening of November 20, 1868, when Judge Orson Brooks, a very old gentleman and respected citizen, who was then police magistrate, was seized by two men at the corner of Sixteenth and Lawrence Streets. One held him while the other rifled his pockets of eighty-six dollars. The robbers were

unfortunate in the accidental choice of their victim, for holding up a police magistrate seemed a special defiance of the law, and besides, although it was dark, Judge Brooks was sure he recognized his assailants.

The city marshal, D. J. Cook, agreed that the description fitted Sam Dugan and Ed Franklin, criminals who were known to be in Denver. Going in search of them, Marshal Cook and Deputy Marshal Haskell found that the two had left town and traced them to Golden. There they found that the men had been spending money freely and drinking even more freely. When the marshals ran Dugan down in a saloon, he met them with a fusillade of revolver shots. A bartender was wounded and Dugan managed to make his escape in the darkness.

Cook then located Franklin in the Overland Hotel in a half-drunken sleep. When he was aroused, Franklin drew his gun. Cook was faster and fired first, killing the outlaw. Franklin was taken to Denver and buried there.

Dugan fled northward toward Cheyenne but was captured and brought back to Denver and locked up in the Larimer Street jail. When his presence there became known, a Vigilante Committee gathered to "handle him." Marshal Cook learned of their plans and, after nightfall on December first, started with the prisoner for a safer place in a stronger building on the west side of town.

At the Larimer Street bridge the Vigilantes intercepted Cook and Dugan, took the prisoner from the officer, and marched him to a tree at the side of Twelfth Street, between Larimer and Market, where they hanged him from a limb. A wagon was drawn up under the tree and Dugan made to stand in it. Then the wagon was pulled from under him. He admitted the Brooks robbery and the killing at Central City, but denied the other crimes he was being credited with. He begged to be allowed to leave the country.

By daylight the news that the Vigilantes had been at work spread over town and photographer Hull hustled down Twelfth Street with the crowd, to take the only picture made of Dugan's body hanging from the tree.

While he was setting up his camera Hull looked up in astonishment to see another man getting ready to make a picture also. It was the deafmute who had stolen Hull's equipment in the mountains. In telling of the hanging of Dugan and describing his dangling body, the *Rocky Mountain News* said:

> We are told certain artists were fighting over it this morning for the exclusive privilege of taking photographic views of it.

If there was an altercation, it was no doubt because of Hull's rightous indignation over his previous experience with the other man, and the only clue as to who won out rests in the fact that Hull's photograph of Dugan is the only one known.

Dugan's body was not removed until ten o'clock in the forenoon. Soon after this episode, the convenient tree was cut down by people living in the vicinity. Dugan was only twenty-three years old, but if he committed all the crimes he was given credit for his had been a busy life.

In the afternon after Dugan's body had been cut down, the Vigilantes took another man, named Musgrove, from the Larimer Street jail. He put up a wild fight with a stick of wood but was hanged from the bridge over Cherry Creek. He was charged with cattle stealing but had a record for murder and had

Sam Dugan, hanged by vigilantes in Denver

been run out of California, Nevada, and Utah by posses. One of the amusing incidents Hull liked to recall, in contrast to the many tragic ones going on at the time, had to do with this man Musgrove. Musgrove first attracted attention in Denver when he appeared with two camels he had stolen from the government on the Mohave Desert. A tenderfoot Englishman shot one, thinking it was an elk and as a result had to endure endless ridicule besides paying for the camel.

Omaha—1869

Back in Omaha about the first of January, 1869, Hull found a new business, Jackson Brothers, Photographers, had opened up the previous summer and he went to work in their studio doing the portrait photography for which he was particularly trained.

William H. Jackson, who is now widely recognized for his sketches, paintings, and photographs of the early West, was a New Yorker, twenty-three years old when he first came to Omaha. He had worked for a photographer in Vermont, coloring photographs, and had learned to sketch and paint in watercolor from his mother. He arrived in Omaha in 1866 and made a trip to California as a bullwhacker, returning the next year as a herder with a drove of half-wild horses. At every opportunity on these trips he made pencil sketches of the scenes that impressed him.

140

These he later translated into watercolor.

In Omaha Jackson secured a job with a photographer named Hamilton, and by the next year Hamilton was willing to sell out to him. Jackson's father was willing to stake him if he would take his brother Edward as a partner. And so Jackson Brothers opened for business in the summer of 1868 at the corner of Fifteenth and Douglas, while Hull was still in the West.

Edward Jackson was the business manager, since he knew accounting and bookkeeping and had had only very brief training in photography. He was struggling with the portrait work, assisted by a young man named Johnson who had come west with him. William Jackson's few months with Hamilton had been a good experience. But he had worked mostly tinting pictures, and he did not like the confinement of the gallery. Both brothers were glad to have Hull appear on the scene. Though Hull had been in the West for two years making outdoor pictures, his earlier experience in his own studio in Minnesota soon brought him back into the swing of portrait work. Both he and Jackson continued to take outdoor scenes, streets and store fronts, sometimes interiors, often on order.

With more freedom, William Jackson fitted up a horse-drawn buggy with a box-like body, which he made into a dark room. With this outfit he drove about the country near Omaha taking pictures of Indians, their lodges and villages. Hull also made Indian pictures and took several short trips into Nebraska on the railroad as it progressed westward, making a collection of negatives which he used later in his own gallery.

It is not hard to imagine that Hull and Jackson had many a bull session that winter, relating their experiences in the West and recalling the beauty of the scenery not yet recorded by camera, examining Jackson's sketches and Hull's photographs. They were both eager to secure with a camera lens, views which perhaps no white man had yet seen, and preserve for all time some of the stirring realities of the westward migration. It was inevitable that they should decide to go back together.

Besides their urge for picture making, Hull and Jackson were, like most young men of the times, fascinated by the railroad building, the great historic and dramatic race against time. They decided to be present when the rails were joined at Promontory in Utah Territory. But it was the first of May before the boys had the chance they were hoping for. Jackson Brothers secured a contract from the Union Pacific Railroad Company for 10,000 stereoscopic views along the new railroad line. William Jackson and Arundel Hull planned a summer's trip on the strength of that order, leaving Edward Jackson in charge of the Omaha gallery. With the contract went passes for the two of them which took care of their transportation, but the young men expected to make their living expenses by making and selling photographs as they traveled.

In preparation for the trip they planned their equipment carefully, profiting by Arundel Hull's previous experience with the portable outfit he carried through the mountains for two years, and from Jackson's experimenting in his cart around Omaha. They assembled everything in two black boxes, instead of one as Hull's had been, because they were to carry, in addition to a standard 8x10 camera, a large cumbersome "stereo" with two brass-barreled Willard lenses, 30x15x15 inches in size. They covered their

141

boxes with black cloth, like Hull's which had to be replaced from time to time, and called one the big black box and the other the small black box. In these boxes was everything necessary, not only for making negatives, but for printing and finishing the prints.

The stereoscopic views Jackson and Hull took that summer in 1869 were to find an enthusiastic market and were good advertising for the Union Pacific. It was the beginning of the tremendous popularity of the first three-dimension pictures, viewed through an optical instrument with a separate lens for each eye so that the result was a double photograph giving depth to the picture. Soon every respectable home had in the parlor, on the marble-topped center table, a stereoscope and sets of pictures, including the scenic wonders of the Union Pacific Route.

The Golden Spike was driven at Promontory Point, Utah, uniting the Union Pacific and Central Pacific Railroads on May 10, 1869, but Hull and Jackson were not there in time to witness the ceremony. They had been delayed by Jackson's marriage. It was May 22 when they boarded the train at Omaha. Jackson

kept a diary during the entire trip of four months, which is now in the possession of the New York Public Library, and of which Jackson allowed this writer to make a copy.

Although the original plan was to go directly to Promontory and work back toward Omaha, at the end of the first twenty-four hours the train had reached Cheyenne and the young men were so attracted by the activity in this two-year-old boom town that they stopped over. They found many people wanted photographs of themselves, their homes, or their establishments, and they sold sixty dollars worth as fast as they could make the pictures. This first trying out of their equipment was somewhat simplified when they ran into an old friend, John Summers, who offered them a room above his store in which to do their work.

Their six days in Cheyenne proved that their equipment was practical as they could make it in the light of Hull's previous experience and with the addition of a tent they bought of Summers. They were confident that they would have no trouble grubstaking themselves by selling photographs and at the same time make the views for the Union Pacific.

Little did they realize the hardships they were to encounter. They visited some of the places Hull had seen two years before and many new ones, but they now had more equipment for the stereo work and a tent and food supplies for longer periods. Before they were through with the summer's work, they had carried this as well as their cooking and sleeping gear on their backs several times, to sites which could be reached in no other way.

Whenever possible the train crews, section hands, and station keepers cooperated to pick them up, with their apparatus, and deposit them a few miles farther on. They were rewarded with photographs of themselves, their crews and locomotives. Two engineers who could be counted on for help operated locomotives number 117 and number 143.

According to Jackson's diary, Hull often did the photographic work alone while Jackson made his now historically valuable sketches. The scenes and notes on color that filled his sketchbooks in later years became a large series of watercolors, forming one of the most valuable historical records of the movement of civilization across the plains.

The tent which the boys bought in Cheyenne did not make a dark enough place to do their developing; so much of the work was done at night or actually inside the big black box with a black cloth over the operator's head and shoulders. A modern kodak fan would be amazed at the complication involved and the skill required to make a successful photograph outdoors in 1869. Albumen paper was silvered in a bath of silver nitrate, then, when dry, fumed with ammonia. The paper was cut to size and a picture printed on it, after which it was washed, toned, fixed in chemical baths, finally dried, trimmed, and mounted on cardboard. Sometime during these processes the wind may have come up and blown dust into everything.

Wet plate glass negatives had to be prepared for each exposure and afterward varnished and retouched. When a sufficient number of prints had been made, the sensitive coating was removed so the plate could be resensitized and reused. Although Jackson did manage to save many pates for himself by sending them back to Omaha, there could have been many more if the two young men had not needed to lighten their load. Hull seemed not so concerned about saving

Building Devil's Gate Bridge over Weber River, 1869

Promontory Point, 1869

negatives, since he already had a collection stored in Omaha which he had made over much the same territory.

If the boys lost or ran out of collodians or silverbaths, days were lost while more was sent out from Omaha or Salt Lake City. When things went well the sale of pictures kept them in funds. But sometimes it rained for days. Once they were held up for want of ten cents worth of acid to make a gold solution. Several times they were down to their last cent and once were actually hungry when needed materials arrived sent out by Edward Jackson by express collect. After several days they got up courage to borrow seven dollars from the baggage master to pay the charges. Luckily he was a man from Jackson's home town. The Jackson business in Omaha was supposed to help William financially if he needed it but seemed to fall down on the job. Hull seemed determined not to use the capital he had cached away in Omaha to start a business of his own. Both were sure the trip would finance itself.

The weather was uncomfortably warm when the boys left Cheyenne, and the newsboy on the train in-

troduced them to a drink called "portable lemonade." This was a package of sugar soaked in citric acid, only needing to be dissolved in water to make a refreshing drink.

The first sight that greeted them when the train pulled into Wasatch, Utah, early in the morning, was a negro hanging from a telegraph pole. He had been hanged for robbery and this may have been Jackson's first sight of a Vigilante hanging, but it was by now an old story to Hull. Among the pictures they took in Wasatch was one of the famous "What Cheer" dining room.

At Weber, a town of twenty or thirty tents, they followed a crowd to one which turned out to be the court room where the first case was being tried by the newly elected officials. A young gambler and his "fair but frail aid" each paid a fine of fifteen dollars for disturbing the peace. The whole proceeding took only five minutes.

Reaching Promontory on June 30, they made photographs of the spot where the rails of the two great roads were joined, and of the tent town. Backtracking to Corinne, Hull found an old friend, a photographer named Crissman, who offered the boys all the

Promontory Point, 1869 — back toward town

conveniences of his canvas-and-board gallery. The heat and dust were unbearable; so the use of a dark room was a godsend, and they made almost a hundred dollars the six days they were in Corinne. Certainly Crissman must have been a generous soul to help two traveling photographers work over his own territory.

Jackson and Hull spent the entire month of July in the vicinity of Great Salt Lake, making short trips from Uintah up Echo and Weber Canyons, and to Salt Lake City. The marvelous scenery in the canyons was an unending source of pleasure to the two young photographers, so much so that they had a hard time deciding which views to take. They made pictures of street scenes, business places, and people in Corinne, Weber, and Blue Creek; and at Uintah of the post office, The Snow Flake, the Eicher family and their home.

In the canyons they photographed the bridge at Devil's Gate, the tunnels, the Thousand Mile Tree, Devil's Slide, Pulpit, Death, Monument, Hanging, Castle, and Needles Rocks and many other scenic spots. According to Jackson's diary, the best pictures they got of Devil's Gate were made by Hull alone.

Once when they were not successful in getting the work train to pick them up for a move of eight miles. It took three trips to carry all their gear up on their backs. It was hot weather in the mountains but they had learned to carry a supply of portable lemonade so that any water could be made palatable. Coffee was sold green and had to be roasted in their campfire and was a serious problem in rainy weather. Once when they were able to buy fresh fruit, for which the Salt Lake valley was already becoming known, they made themselves sick feasting on apples, peaches, and watermelon at one sitting.

Going from Uintah to Salt Lake, they took the stagecoach of the "Opposition Line" at three dollars instead of the Wells Fargo coach at five dollars. In the city they furbished themselves up to look respectable and went to the theater two or three times, once to see Anne Ward in a comedy. Hull took a forbidden photograph of the Mormon Tabernacle while Jackson kept the caretaker busy. They also got a picture of Brigham's Wall and a number of views about the city, including one down Main Street from the hill.

148

Promontory, Utah Territory, 1869

Scene at Promontory, 1869

On September 19 there was a flurry of snow and the mountain tops were white. Jackson was becoming more and more worried about the condition of the Omaha business and decided to return there. He impatiently waited for a pass to Omaha which finally came so that he could board the train on September 28. Hull remained to dispose of some of the equipment and to pack the rest. Taking several weeks to get back to Omaha, he spent some time in Columbus and Fremont, Nebraska, considering a location for a gallery. He then continued to Omaha and worked once more in the Jackson gallery until the end of the year. Then he went to Fremont to start a business of his own.

Arundel C. Hull, Photographer, opened his gallery for business in a new building he had built at 331 Main Street, Fremont, Nebraska, on January 1, 1870.

It was assuredly one of the first, and may have been the first, permanent photographic business in Nebraska outside of Omaha. The business was leased to Fritz and Good in 1893 or 1894 and was later operated by Fritz alone for many years. The business changed hands several times, but the building remained the property of the Hull family until it was torn down in 1928. It remained a sort of landmark to many old timers who refered to it as the "Old Hull Gallery."

In 1873 Arundel C. Hull married Florence C. Miller, daughter of Alanson Miller and Charlotte Marshall Miller. Of their six children, the writer was the youngest, born when most of the rest had reached adulthood. None of the five is now alive to read this tribute to their father's memory.

SOURCES

History of the State of Nebraska, 1882. Western Historical Company

History of Nebraska. J. Sterling Morton

History of Omaha, 1866-1869. Savage and Bell

The Story of Omaha. Sorenson

The History of Omaha, 1889. Sorenson

Pacific Tourist Guide, 1885. Ed. F. E. Shearer

Wolfe's *U.P.R.R. Gazetter*, 1875-1875

How We Built the Union Pacific Railroad. Major General Grenville M. Dodge

The Indian War of 1864. Eugene F. Ware

Pioneer Heros and Heroines, 1888. Frank Triplett

History of Denver. Jerome Smiley

History of Larimer County. Watrous

History of Colorado, 1889, Vol. I. Frank Hall

Personal Diary, 1869. William H. Jackson

A Pioneer Denver Mint, 1860-1865. Noley Mumey

American Rifleman, February, 1951. John J. Bersotti

History of Wyoming. Coutant

History and Directory of Laramie City. J. H. Triggs

History of Cheyenne. J. H. Triggs

History of Wyoming. State Historians

Turner's Guide to the Rocky Mountains, 1868.

Personal Recollections of Pioneer Life. Luke Vorhees

Wyoming. State Historians

Frontier Days. Judge Kuykendall

Annals of Wyoming. State Historians

Fifty Years on the Trail, John Y. Nelson

Fremont (Nebraska) *Herald,* 1870-1900

Frontier Index on microfilm:
    March 6, 24, 1868
    May 20, 22, 26, 1868
    June 6, 1868
    Aug. 11, 1868
    Sept. 11, 20, 1868

Cheyenne Leader—original newspapers:
    Jan. 4, 9, 1867
    Oct. 12, 15, 17, 1867
    Nov. 16, 1867
    April 25, 1868
    May 5, 26, 1868
    June 20, 1868
    Aug. 10, 15, 19, 1868

Family papers and letters, and family reminiscences